PATIENCE IN ISLAM
SABR

Tallal Alie Turfe

Published by
Tahrike Tarsile Qur'an, Inc.
Publishers and Distributors of Holy Qur'an
P.O. Box 731115
Elmhurst, New York 11373-0115

Published by
Tahrike Tarsile Qur'an, Inc.
Publishers and Distributors of Holy Qur'an
P.O. Box 731115
Elmhurst, New York 11373-0115

First U.S. Edition

Library of Congress Catalog Number: 96-60267
Copyright © 1996 Tallal Alie Turfe
British Library Cataloguing in Publication Data

ISBN: 1-879402-32-7

Distributors in U.K. and Europe:
Murtaza Bandali/ALIF International
37 Princes Avenue
Watford, Herts WD1 7RR
England, U.K.

PATIENCE IN ISLAM
SABR

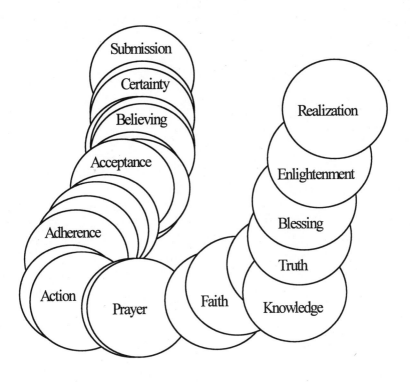

Tallal Alie Turfe, Professor
at the
University of Michigan

CONTENTS

PREFACE

"...O my Lord! My Lord! My Lord! Strengthen my limbs for Thy service and sustain my strength and perseverance to continue it. (Lord) Grant me that I may continuously endeavor to keep Thy fear (in my mind) and to be occupied constantly in Thy service...." (al-Imam Ali, Dua-e-Kumail)

This book is written for the beginning students of Islam in search for an understanding of the fundamental aspects of Islam, as well as for the more advanced students who wish to broaden their Islamic perspective. In addition, non-Muslims wishing to learn about the religion of Islam will find this book of interest.

This book is dedicated to my parents, Hajj Alie and Hajji Hassaney Turfe, who were constant and steadfast in their faith and good deeds. To my sister, Hajji Wanda Fayz, and my wife, Hajji Neemat Turfe, whose humanitarian efforts have comforted those in need and whose determination for Islamic unity in our community has been a major contribution. To my sister-in-law, Elizabeth Turfe, whose example in attitude and behavior was an inspiration to me to begin and complete this book. She so patiently persevered in nursing my late brother, Hajj Fouad Turfe, for over twenty years as he was bedridden with multiple sclerosis, and never once did she complain.

Each of us goes through life wanting to understand more clearly our metaphysical relationship with Allah. In search of knowledge and wisdom, we broaden our horizons and equip ourselves with the tools to help fulfill this mission. As we strive towards self-actualization, we find ourselves thirsty and eager to learn even more about Islam. This book will enlighten those who wish to reflect on Islam and its fundamental principles, with particular focus on one of Islam's most powerful concepts--sabr (patience)!

I would like to thank the dedicated Muslim scholars who had read this book and provided counsel with their comments. Their contribution to this book is in the way of Allah only, as they do not seek recognition by name. May Allah shower them with His Blessings.

Tallal Alie Turfe

5

ABOUT THE AUTHOR

Tallal Alie Turfe was born in Detroit, Michigan on April 19, 1940. He is the son of Hajj Alie Turfe and Hajji Hassaney Turfe. He has four brothers (Bennett, Hajj Fouad, Feisal, and Atallah) and one sister, Hajji Wanda Fayz. His wife is Hajji Neemat Turfe, and they have four sons (Alie, Norman, Robert, and Hassan) and one daughter (Summer). Two of his sons graduated from the United States Military Academy at West Point. This achievement is a first for a Muslim to have entered and graduated from that Academy. That institution has produced the greatest American generals, and it also was the school from where some of America's presidents graduated.

Currently, Tallal is employed by General Motors Corporation in the area of Strategic Marketing. Previously, he had been Director of Trade Relations for General Motors Corporation. In that capacity, his responsibilities were to oversee countertrade activities throughout Europe, Middle East, and Africa. Additionally, he is a Professor at several universities such as the University of Michigan, Wayne State University, Eastern Michigan University, Central Michigan University, and the University of Windsor (Canada). On a part-time basis, since 1969, he has taught mostly graduate courses in the field of business administration with concentration primarily in the disciplines of marketing, management, and business policy.

Tallal serves as Chairman of the Arab-American and Chaldean Council, a social services agency which renders assistance to Arabs and Chaldeans in the tri-county area of Michigan (Wayne, Macomb, and Oakland counties). With twenty-two centers, it provides services in the areas of job training, mental health, substance abuse, teen counseling, school counseling, immigration, English as a second language, and a multitude of other social services.

In addition, Tallal also serves as Co-Chairman of the Greater Detroit Interfaith Round Table, National Conference. This organization helps build bridges between the various religious faiths, and it helps in securing peace and harmony among the various ethnic groups in the Detroit Metropolitan communities. He is also a board member of the Citizens Council for Michigan Public Universities, and he is a member of the American Task Force for Lebanon.

Tallal has also been instrumental in securing gainful employment for thousands of Muslim and non-Muslim immigrants primarily from the Middle East. For this achievement, a testimonial dinner was given in his honor by his community in February of 1974.

7

Another testimonial dinner was given in his honor in October of 1995 as he was presented with the "Knights of Charity Award" by the Pontifical Institute for Foreign Missions, an international community of Christian priests and lay missionaries who "maintain a preferential and evangelical option for the poor and marginalized of society."

Frequently, Tallal gives lectures on Islam in various mosques and churches located in the Detroit Metropolitan area. For thirteen years, he conducted religious classes at the Islamic Center of America (previously Islamic Center of Detroit). In addition, for the past ten years, he has been a lecturer on Islam at the Islamic Institute of Knowledge, located in Dearborn, Michigan. He has published several articles on Islam.

In the Name of Allah, the Beneficent, the Merciful

PATIENCE

by Tallal Alie Turfe

Patience is a virtue I'll try to explain,
A blessing in disguise always to remain.
From very deep inside the well of my heart,
Peace of body and mind and the will to start.
I'm summoned by a call at the dawn of day,
Just giving thanks to Him as I kneel to pray.
Endurance is my counsel and faith my guide,
The door is open to the struggle inside.
With knowledge of certainty, I now can see,
The reality of truth, plain as can be.
It is charity that gives meaning to life,
From the love of my caring in times of strife.
Piety and wisdom help me through the day,
But always I will return to kneel and pray.
For it is patience, the essence of my goal,
That enlightens and gives meaning to my soul.

PART I: SABR: AN ISLAMIC PERSPECTIVE

Need for Sabr

Muslims throughout the world continue to search for knowledge, understanding, and wisdom in order to learn as much as they can about the religion of Islam. From time to time they deter from that cause by falling prey to the desires and evils of this world. Lack of education in Islam keeps them short of ever self-actualizing themselves as complete Muslims. What is needed is a mechanism by which they can be assured that their faith will be complete and secure. The mechanism needed to bind the tie between the ideological aspects (Articles of Faith) and practical aspects (Branches of Faith) of Islam is *sabr* (patience).

Except for Allah, never has a word or concept ever had such a dramatic impact on our daily lives as does sabr. Sabr is derived from one of the many attributes of Allah. Sabr enables us to fulfill our purpose in life. Without it, we are like nomads in the desert searching for water to quench our thirst but never realizing that the well is just beneath our feet.

Definition of Sabr

Sabr is not easily translated into English. Sabr takes on many characteristics. It means not only patience but also constancy, endurance, perseverance, self-restraint, forbearance, and steadfastness. (Figure 1, p. 18)

The essence of the definition of sabr is when people restrain themselves from committing evil, obey Allah's Orders by holding their hearts firm, and refrain from complaining about anything bad that happens to them. The best example of sabr is when people, who are faced with calamity and adversity, hold steadfast in their sabr and place their trust in Allah.

Binding Tie

Sabara, the verb form of sabr, means to bind or tie. What we bind or tie are our weaknesses and irrational behavior that can taint, demean, and destroy our Islamic personality. We bind these deficiencies through control of our thoughts and desires.

To bind or tie takes yet another meaning. It is that meaning which forms the thesis for this research. Sabr becomes the binding tie between the Articles of Faith (*Usul al-Din*) and the Branches of Faith (*Furu' al-Din*). (Figure 2, p. 19)

There are three major categories of the Articles of Faith:
1. Belief in Allah

11

2. Belief in the Prophets
3. Belief in the Hereafter

The Belief in the Unity of Allah, the Justice of Allah, the Angels, the Imamah (succession of Prophet Mohammad), and the Books of Allah derive from these three categories. For example, the Books of Allah are revealed to the Prophets who in turn deliver Allah's Divine Revelation to mankind.

The Branches of Faith are many. Some of them are:

1. Prayer
2. Fasting
3. Alms
4. Pilgrimage
5. Struggle (*Jihad*)

Definition of Islam

Looking at these two aspects of faith, we need to arrive at a definition of Islam. Al-Imam Ali (first cousin and son-in-law of Prophet Mohammad, and a Caliph of Islam) eloquently described Islam by stating:

"Islam is submission; submission is certainty; certainty is believing; believing is acceptance; acceptance is adherence; adherence is action."

As a student of al-Imam Ali, and guided by his maxims and sermons, I have included the words *attitude, endurance, behavior*, and *patience* in this definition: (Figure 3, p. 20)

"Islam is attitude, the zenith of which is endurance; endurance is submission; submission is certainty; certainty is believing; believing is acceptance; acceptance is adherence; adherence is action; action is behavior, the essence of which is patience."

Significance of Certainty

It is the certainty in the definition of Islam which has a special meaning. Three levels of certainty are described: (Figure 4, p. 21)

1. Knowledge of certainty (*'ilm al-yakine*)
2. Perception of certainty (*'ain al-yakine*)
3. Truth of certainty (*haq al-yakine*)

"Nay, were ye to know with certainty of mind, (ye would beware!) Ye shall certainly see Hell-fire! Again, ye shall see it with certainty of sight!" (Qur'an 102:5-7)

"But verily it is truth of assured certainty." (Qur'an 69:51)

Let us look at some examples of these levels of certainty:

Knowledge of Certainty:

With knowledge, one has certainty of mind. Reason and information guide us to knowledge. We see clouds or smoke and believe with certainty that rain may be forthcoming or there is a fire. Conscience is also a source of knowledge. We must condition and instruct our minds towards the righteous path, thereby rendering our conscience as clear and pure.

Perception of Certainty:

We now see the rain or fire. Another example is that of punishment. If we do not use our minds towards the good deeds, we shall surely perceive and see the certainty of punishment - the inevitable Hell! We must feel and be inspired by the words of Allah. We must see the clear path by seeking knowledge, understanding, and wisdom by way of Allah's Revelations.

Truth of Certainty:

Truth is in itself certain. Here, at the highest level of certainty, there can be no error of knowing or error of seeing. There is a form of spiritual and actual union that exists between the knower and the known thing. Not only is there rain or fire, but we can actually touch the rain or feel the warmth of the fire. The assurance of the Hereafter is truth. And truth will prevail. Reaching this highest level of certainty, the certainty of truth, one must have the capacity to receive and understand the truth, be free of sin, be free of worldly interests, and be free of prejudice. This level of certainty is one of the highest levels possible for man.

To achieve any of these three levels of certainty takes a great deal of patience (sabr). This achievement is not automatic; it takes a great deal of effort and concentration. According to Prophet Mohammad:

"Certainty is complete belief."

With sabr one moves quickly from one level of certainty to the next. Steadfastness (sabr) wins the pleasure of Allah. Steadfastness is more than a miracle. There is a constant need to be steadfast whether in good times or bad times. For example, assume that one is encircled by calamities, and his life, honor, and good name are all in peril with no means of comfort available, that even visions and dreams and revelations are suspended by Allah as a trial, and he is left helpless among terrible dangers. At such a time, one should not lose heart nor retreat like a coward, nor let one's faithfulness be put in doubt in the least. One should not let one's sincerity and perseverance be weakened. This is the steadfastness which leads to the devotion of Allah.

13

Conditions for Submission

Before one can submit, he or she must first have the attitude or frame of mind to be ready to take hold of the banner of Islam. All the other criteria in the definition of Islam will now fall into place. When we have the attitude to endure as Muslims, and action translates into patience by way of behavior and example, the end result is a bullet-proof, impregnable, definition.

Sabr becomes one of the most important aspects in our daily lives. In short, sabr transcends into what we call *taqwah* (consciousness of Allah). Thereafter, everything we do is *kurbatan illallah*, that is, to become nearer to Allah. Without sabr, we are like a ship lost at sea never knowing which direction to turn. Sabr is the compass that directs and guides us to the straight path. Without sabr, the Articles of Faith are minimized, one's faith is weakened, the unity of Allah is distorted, the books of Allah merely points of reference, the angels only guides, the prophets no more than messengers, and resurrection a dimensional sphere. Without sabr, the Branches of Faith are likewise minimized as prayer becomes only words, fasting a time constraint, pilgrimage a formality, charity a sympathetic gesture, and struggle a reaction.

Sabr (Hidden Sense)

Basically, humans have five senses: smell, taste, touch, sound, and sight. There is another sense: the hidden sense of sabr. While we take the other senses for granted and pay little attention to them unless they become impaired, the sense of sabr is latent and needs to be brought to the surface. This requires a great deal of effort, oftentimes a "second effort." (Figure 5, p. 22)

People often give up too easily, become lazy, and become victimized by boredom. They lack the quality that will enable them to reach their potential as human beings. They strike out too soon. Actually, trying a little harder, attempting another effort, may be all that is needed to reach this hidden sense of sabr. The weak person fails to try, to persevere in the face of laziness, because he feels that continued effort would only result in failure. He does not realize that persistency can result in success. Remember that it is easy to give up, to be too tired to make the "second effort."

It often has been said that one should not quit until every possibility has been exhausted, but it may be that he exhausts his few possibilities too quickly. He may have equipped himself with so little ammunition that he soon runs out and has nothing left with which to persevere. Possibly, lack of perseverance is not lack of inclination but

14

lack of preparation. What preparation is needed here is to equip oneself with the knowledge, understanding, and wisdom of Islam and, equally important, to begin the effort of practicing Islam to the fullest extent. If one is properly prepared, and if one has the determination and confidence to succeed, he will persevere until he successfully brings to surface the sense of sabr.

Virtues in Islam

Sabr is the anchor of four key virtues in Islam: (Figure 6, p. 23)

"By time (through the ages), verily man is in a state of loss, except those who believe and do good deeds, and who direct each other to the truth and who direct each other to patience (sabr)." (Qur'an 103:1-3)

It is reported that Prophet Mohammad had said that the aforementioned chapter (*Al-Asr*), comprised of fourteen Arabic words, constitutes one-third of the meaning of the entire Qur'an. These are the four virtues of Islam. And honor (*sharaf*) is the tribute we pay to virtue. Honor is a recognition of faith, good deeds, truth, and patience. When we honor people, the honor comes not from us but from them, from that which they reflect in their lives. We are honored in honoring them.

Honor is an admonition to us to go and do likewise, in hard times as well as in easy times, in great moments--but above all in small moments, in moments unseen and unknown. When? Now! Now is the time to redeem the time, now is the time for faith, good deeds, truth, and patience.

Unity in Islam

In today's society, we are constantly faced with challenges and threats by those who want to destroy Islam. With unity in diversity, we can utilize the shield of sabr to thwart off any temptation, threat, weakness, passion, or fear:

"So have sabr! Verily your sabr is from Allah, and do not let yourself be grieved or distressed because of their deceptions." (Qur'an 16:127)

Sabr strengthens the rope of Allah and binds the Muslims together as one:

"And hold fast to the rope of Allah and be not divided."(Qur'an 3:103)

This bind or tie manifests itself in sabr. Muslims unify for the common goal of serving Allah. With sabr, unity will be achieved. We note that the word sabr usually precedes the pillars of Islam as well as

15

concepts which form our Islamic foundation. For example, we note the terms sabr and prayer, sabr and struggle, sabr and faith, and sabr and comfort. The importance of sabr is emphasized by its position at the beginning of the phrase. In each situation, sabr strengthens and reinforces the other concept. For example, what good is *salwan* (comfort) in times of bereavement if the comforter has no sabr (patience)? Likewise, how can one truly defend the religion of Islam against evil if the spirit of *jihad* (struggle) does not translate into sabr (endurance and constancy).

Highest Level of Sabr

The pinnacle of sabr is reached when one is completely absorbed by it:

"To have patience with patience is the highest level of beauty." *(Qur'an 70:5)*

Reaching the *highest level of beauty* now means reaching the *highest level of excellence.* (Figure 7, p. 24)

Not many self-actualize to this level of "patience with patience," but it is our constant goal to strive towards it. Although the prophets had reached this level, there were others. For example, during the time of Prophet Mohammad great Muslim martyrs, such as Yassir and Somaya, and their son, Ammar, as well as Miqdad, Abu-Dhar, and Salman al-Farsi, attained this level. Here are examples of where sabr is also associated with calamities and difficulties as well as tests. Hardships may befall us, and it is our perseverance which will carry us through these disasters and misfortunes.

It should be realized that in times of misfortune and hardship, Allah causes a light to descend upon the hearts of those He loves by strengthening them with great serenity. A true believer moves forward under misfortunes and submits completely to the Will of Allah. For Allah teaches us that the sufferings which He imposes upon us are a means of perfecting our knowledge through experience. The ultimate certainty of knowledge is achieved through experience of every part of it.

Concept of Patience in Islam

In Islam, the concept of patience (sabr) is one of action. (Figure 8, p. 25)

For Muslims, patience is proactive rather than reactive. It is a time to perform. This performance may be the length of time one can persevere even in the face of calamity and difficulty.

In Islam, patience is attained through effort. This effort is not automatic, rather, it takes a great deal of concentration and control of

16

one's inner self. We must strive in the way of Islam, and that way is achieved through a concerted and genuine effort by each of us. We must make the effort to obtain sabr, for it is sabr that becomes the "key of relief" (*miftah al-faraj*).

Sabr: A Methodological Framework

Simplified, the methodology begins with a definition of Islam which transcends into what constitutes faith, virtues, and the laws of Islam. Special emphasis is given to the concepts of attitude and behavior as they are the pivotal points in preparing Muslims to self-actualize to the level of sabr. How one is guided and enlightened is his ability to seek knowledge by use of the powers of the human soul as he submits to the will of Allah and seeks His Blessing. (Figure 9, p. 26)

FIGURE 1

CHARACTERISTICS OF SABR

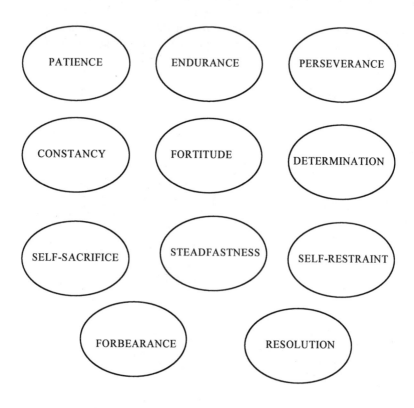

SOURCE: TALLAL ALIE TURFE

FIGURE 2

SABR:
THE BINDING TIE

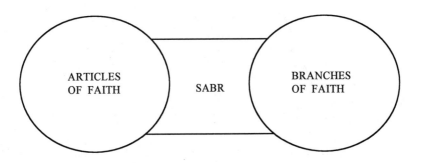

SOURCE: TALLAL ALIE TURFE

FIGURE 3

DEFINITION OF ISLAM

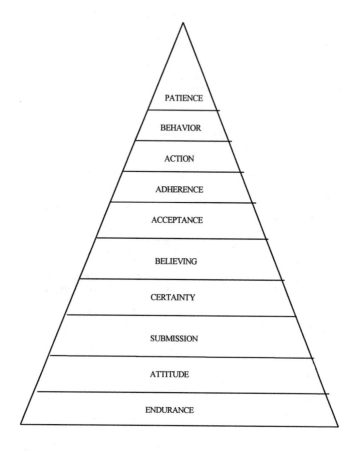

SOURCES: AL-IMAM ALI; TALLAL ALIE TURFE

FIGURE 4

SABR AND CERTAINTY

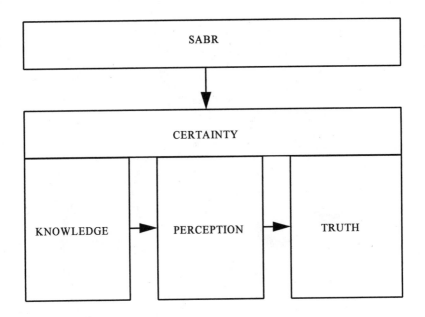

SOURCE: QUR'AN 56:95; 69:51; 102:5-7

FIGURE 5

SABR - HIDDEN SENSE

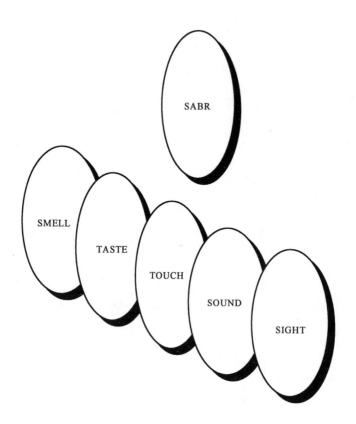

SOURCE: TALLAL ALIE TURFE

FIGURE 6

VIRTUES IN ISLAM

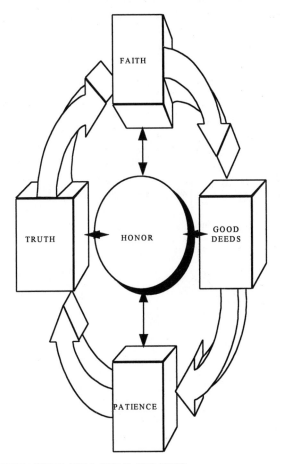

SOURCES: QUR'AN 103:1-3; TALLAL ALIE TURFE

FIGURE 7

SABR

PATIENCE WITH PATIENCE
(HIGHEST LEVEL OF BEAUTY AND EXCELLENCE)

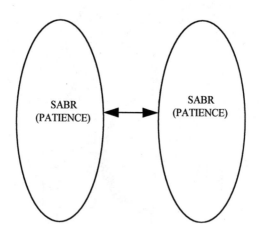

SOURCE: QUR'AN 70:5

FIGURE 8

CONCEPT OF PATIENCE (SABR)
IN ISLAM

WHAT IT IS
• ACTIVE
• PROACTIVE

WHAT IT IS NOT
• PASSIVE
• REACTIVE

SOURCE: TALLAL ALIE TURFE

25

FIGURE 9

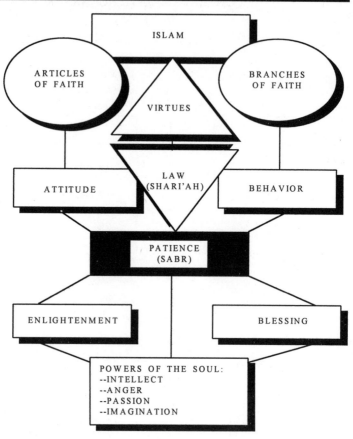

SABR:
A METHODOLOGICAL FRAMEWORK

ISLAM

ARTICLES
OF FAITH

BRANCHES
OF FAITH

VIRTUES

LAW
(SHARI'AH)

ATTITUDE

BEHAVIOR

PATIENCE
(SABR)

ENLIGHTENMENT

BLESSING

POWERS OF THE SOUL:
--INTELLECT
--ANGER
--PASSION
--IMAGINATION

SOURCE: TALLAL ALIE TURFE

26

PART II: ISLAMIC THEOLOGY OF SABR

A. Articles of Faith

Belief in Allah

Sabr is secondary when used in conjunction with Allah:

"Have sabr for the sake of your Lord." (Qur'an 74:7)

Here we see that the practice of sabr would greatly please Allah. In fact, *as-Sabur* (derived from sabr) is one of the attributes and names of Allah, and it means "The Patient." Sabr of Allah is different than sabr of human beings. Whenever we say Sabr of Allah, it means that Allah will be Patient by giving His Mercy even to those who repent and seek Allah's Forgiveness. Allah related to Prophet David (Dawood) that he must attain the highest level of patience, ethics, and morality:

"Have patience at what they say, and remember Our servant, David, the man of strength: for he ever turned (to Allah)." (Qur'an 38:17)

Likewise, Prophet Mohammad followed the highest level of patience, ethics, and morality in the way of Allah. To be patient in all matters is the best advice, and Allah sent Prophet Mohammad as an example of patience. Allah had ordered Prophet Mohammad to be patient:

"And We shall try you until We test those among you who strive their utmost and persevere in patience; and We shall try your reported (mettle)." (Qur'an 47:31)

When Prophet Mohammad displays the best in patience, others will follow the Prophet's example. Whomever displays the best in patience are the patient ones. Allah knows who are the best in the way of patience, and He knows when people exercise patience in the face of adversity and in the face of negative remarks by others towards them. Allah also knows the sadness the patient ones endure during these difficult times.

Allah was Patient when He created the heavens and the earth in six terms or periods. Allah could have done it in a day, a minute, a second, or less than a second. But He displayed the example of Patience by performing this task in that time period.

The Beautiful Names of Allah (*Al-Asmau'l-Husna*):

Ninety-nine (99) names of Allah can be found in the Qur'an: (Figure 10, p. 47)

27

"Say: 'Call Him Allah or Rahman (Beneficent): By whatever name ye call upon Him, (it is well): for to Him belong the Most Beautiful Names....'" (Qur'an 17:110)

Note that one of the names is *as-Sabur* ("The Patient"). If we add the name of Allah to the list, the total is one-hundred. In addition, some *ulama* (religious scholars) add the name *Rab* ("Lord"). Since "God" and "Lord" are English names, they do not appear in the Qur'an, which is written in the Arabic language. It is interesting to note that some religious scholars (from the monotheistic faiths) have related that He has as many as three thousand names.

Throughout the Qur'an, Allah reminds us of sabr:

"We sent Moses with Our Signs (and the command). 'Bring out Thy people from the depths of darkness into light, and teach them to remember the Days of Allah.' Verily in this there are Signs for such as are firmly patient and constant - grateful and appreciative." (Qur'an 14:5)

"But indeed if any show patience and forgive, that would truly be an exercise of courageous will and resolution in the conduct of affairs." (Qur'an 42:43)

Rather than punish the guilty, it is a far more difficult task to be patient and forgive. This act of patience and forgiveness is the highest level of courage and resolution. To demonstrate by example one's patience and forgiveness may be the panacea for restoring a violator back to righteousness or at the least normalcy in the society.

Allah is Omnipotent (All-Powerful) Omniscient (All-Knowing), and Omnipresent (Everywhere). What is with Allah endures:

"What is with you must vanish: what is with Allah will endure. And We will certainly bestow, on those who patiently persevere, their reward according to the best of their actions." (Qur'an 16:96)

Whatever good actions one does will always remain with Allah, and Allah will reward according to one's best action, not according to one's merit or potential. If one's potential is to do better, then that person is rewarded by Allah for what one does, not for what one can do.

Devotion to Allah:

Through our own individual self-refinement (*tazkiya*) of our souls, we secure our faith through *ikhlas* (devotion to Allah). Our reliance (*tawakkul*) on Allah guides us to the straight path and manifests itself in seeking Allah's Contentment (*Qana'a*), Gratitude (*Shukr*), Generosity (*Infaq*), and Patience (*Sabr*). We seek *tawakkul* by complete obedience to

Him. This obedience takes the shape of piety (*taqwah*), love, and loyalty to Allah. For us, sabr begins with our steadfastness in belief, to resist temptations and inferior desires, and to be firm in hardship and difficulties. Allah tests our faith. How we score on these tests determines the extent of our devotion to Allah. Assurance of the highest score on these tests can be achieved through one's faith, righteous deeds, truth, and patience. (Figure 6, p. 23; Figure 11, p. 48)

With man's self-refinement of his soul, heart, and mind, Allah will reward him in the Hereafter:

"And because they were patient and constant, He will reward them with a Garden and (garments) of silk." (Qur'an 76:12)

Seek Allah's Contentment, Gratitude, Generosity, and Patience by persevering in your own constancy:

"Therefore, be patient with constancy to the Command of thy Lord, and hearken not to the sinner or the ingrate among them." (Qur'an 76:24)

And the Command is to be obedient to Allah. How we reach the level of obedience is through adherence to Islam by way of the example of Prophet Mohammad:

"And obey Allah and His Apostle; and fall into no disputes, lest ye lose heart and your power depart; and be patient and persevering; for Allah is with those who patiently persevere." (Qur'an 8:46)

Sabr and Faith

"....those who fear Allah; who believe in the Unseen, are steadfast in prayer, and spend out of what We have provided for them; and who believe in the Revelation sent to thee, and sent before thy time, and (in their hearts) have the assurance of the Hereafter. They are on (true) guidance, from their Lord, and it is these who will prosper...." (Qur'an 2:2-7)

Interaction of Faith and Sabr:

Al-Imam Ali had said:

"Practice endurance (sabr); it is to faith what the head is to the body. There is no good in a body without a head, or in faith without endurance."

A body is useless without a head, since it is the brain which is the chief mechanism for sustaining life. Likewise faith is useless without endurance, since belief must be sustainable throughout one's entire life. Faith by itself is idealistic; with endurance it becomes realistic and

29

actionable. Being steadfast in prayer, for example, guides the pious Muslim to the straight path.

Through the best of times as well as the worst of times, we strive to perfect ourselves through sabr. While wealth and prosperity are great blessings, they are also, at the same time, great trials of faith:

"And if We cause him (man) to taste of great blessing after some misfortune which has befallen him, he says: 'ills have departed from me.' Lo, he becomes exultant and boastful, except for those who have sabr and do good works. Theirs will be forgiveness and a great reward." (Qur'an 11:10-11)

Allah guides us to the straight path and overlooks our shortcomings. When we turn to Allah for guidance, we are protected from those who are deceived by complacency and materialistic gains of this world. Sabr has its roots in a deep-seated faith, which results in displaying the best attitude and best behavior. How well we perform is determined by tests which Allah has provided:

"Or do you think that you will enter Paradise without tests like those who came before you? They encountered suffering and adversity; and were shaken in spirit that even the Prophet and those of faith who were with him cried: 'When (will come) the help of Allah?' Ah! Verily, the help of Allah is (always) near!" (Qur'an 2:214)

Danger of Compromising Islam:

Compromising Islam occurs throughout the world irrespective of geographical location. Many people bring innovations into Islam that are strictly cultural practices and then proceed to label them as Islamic. This phenomenon occurs in all societies. There can be no compromising the laws of Islam. Islam is a path or ideology in and of itself; the divine plan of Allah. As Muslims, we should begin to make it a practice to use Islam as Allah's Criteria for us in regards to tradition. Compromised Islam is not Islam, but a man-made ideology. With Islam as our standard, we can judge whether or not a practice is appropriate and act accordingly. This practice unites the people (*ummah*) under the banner of Islam wherever they live.

Should Muslims compromise their Islamic values and ideals, they would fall into the lowest form of degradation for they would have substituted Islam for convenience and social compatibility:

"They wish to deceive Allah and the believers, but they do not deceive anyone except themselves, but they realize it not." (Qur'an 2:9)

Truly, their resolve is being tested. Once the believer has control over his internal and external self, and sabr becomes the guiding light of his faith, then he is ready to face all tests and trials with an open mind, open heart, and confidence. The main objective of those who label you as a non-conformist is to deter you from Islam:

"They will not stop fighting you until they turn you back from your religion, if they can." (Qur'an 2:217)

Look to sabr as your salvation, and do not be fooled by the deception, hypocrisy, and disbelief that surrounds you:

"So have patience! For your patience is from Allah, and do not let yourself be grieved or distressed because of their deceptions." (Qur'an 16:127)

Strengthen your ties with Islam and increase your faith through endurance and determination:

"So persevere with sabr, for verily the promise of Allah is true, and do not let those grieve you who have no certainty of faith." (Qur'an 30:60)

Complementation of Faith and Good Deeds:

One strengthens his faith through practicing good deeds. Al-Imam Ali said:

"Faith leads you to good deeds and good deeds lead you to faith."

Complementary in perspective, faith and good deeds reinforce each other and as such bring out the best in sabr. Oftentimes, good deeds are nullified as one boasts about his achievements. With sabr, one quietly performs his good deed and seeks his only reward from the good in having performed that deed:

"Is there any reward for good other than good?" (Qur'an 55:60)

Nothing can define good better than good. Therefore, one is rewarded for his good deeds with the good in having done them.

When you submit your will to Allah, be certain of your faith, believe in the unity of Allah, accept the challenge that you will strive in the way of Allah to better yourself as a Muslim, and constantly adhere to Allah's Commands. Be steadfast and actionable in your obligation to Islam. Display the right attitude so that your faith can endure. Let your example and behavior be one for others to follow, and above all be patient:

31

"Follow thou the inspiration sent unto thee, and be patient and constant, till Allah does decide: for He is the Best to decide." (Qur'an 10:109)

What can better express the inspiration but the lamp of patience, that sovereign virtue for those who have faith. And for this we make our declaration of faith (*shahadah*):

"I bear witness that there is no God but Allah and that Mohammad is His Messenger."

This is the first duty of a Muslim. This confession of faith has two parts: declaration of the absolute oneness of Allah and the prophethood of Mohammad. A submission to anyone other than Allah is a breach of faith. In addition, a denial of the message of Prophet Mohammad is likewise a breach of faith. Once we utter the *shahadah*, we declare ourselves as Muslims. As Muslims, it is incumbent upon us to recite the Qur'an and to follow the example of Prophet Mohammad.

Sabr and Allah's Books

The Books (*Kutub*) of Allah are revealed in the Ultimate Book (*Qur'an*):

"This is the Book; in it is guidance sure, without doubt, to those who fear Allah." (Qur'an 2:2)

"Those to whom We have sent the Book study it as it should be studied; they are the ones that believe therein: those who reject faith therein - the loss is their own." (Qur'an 2:121)

Qur'an:

The Qur'an was revealed to Prophet Mohammad through the Angel Gabriel, to reassure Allah's Benevolence and Mercy and to correct the misinterpretations of His previous Books revealed to other Messengers:

"And We sent down the Book to thee for the express purpose, that thou shouldst make clear to them those things in which they differ, and that it should be a guide and a mercy to those who believe." (Qur'an 16:64)

The Books were sent for the express purpose of unifying the various sects, to teach the right conduct, and to guide man towards salvation. The sects had fallen in disarray and were leading a very dangerous path.

Other Books of Allah - the Torah (*Taurat*), the Psalms (*Zuboor*), and the Gospel (*Injeel*) - were revealed in stages. (Figure 12, p. 49)

32

"It is He Who sent down to thee (step by step), in truth, the Book, confirming what went before it; and He sent down the Law (of Moses) and the Gospel (of Jesus) before this, as a guide to mankind, and He sent down the Criterion (of judgment between right and wrong). " (Qur'an 3:3)

"We have sent thee Inspiration, as We sent it to Noah and the Messengers after him: We sent Inspiration to Abraham, Ismail, Isaac, Jacob and the Tribes, to Jesus, Job, Jonah, Aaron, and Solomon, and to David We gave the Psalms. " (Qur'an 4:163)

Occurrence of Sabr in the Qur'an:

The word sabr and its derivatives occur 103 times in the Qur'an. (Appendix) It was by Allah's Design that sabr would be strategically situated throughout the Qur'an as a guidance for the reader.

There are forty-five chapters which contain the word sabr. This constitutes forty percent (40%) of the total number of chapters (114). The chapters containing the most occurrences of sabr are: Chapter 2: *Baqara* (9), Chapter 3: *Al-i-Imran* (8), Chapter 18: *Kahf* (8), and Chapter 16: *Nahl* (7). These four chapters constitute about one-third of the total number of occurrences of sabr in the Qur'an. There are ninety-three (93) verses that contain the word sabr, and ten of these verses each contain the word sabr twice.

The most frequent derivative of sabr is *isbir* (19 times) followed by *sabaru* (15 times) and *alsabireen* (15 times). About one-half of the total occurrences of sabr is the result of these three derivatives: *isbir, sabaru,* and *alsabireen.*

Sabr in Other Books:

While sabr occurs very often in the Torah and Gospel, we cannot know exactly what is Divine Revelation as these Books have been modified from the original form. Therefore, it is only important to state that sabr occurs very often in these Books; however, the extent of its occurrence cannot be justified.

Sabr and Angels

Description of Angels:

Some angels (*malaika*) have two wings (one pair) or many pairs of wings. There is no precise number or pair of wings. The two, or three, or four (pairs) indicates a continuance and may number tens, hundreds, or some other number. According to al-Imam Ali, Allah created angels in various shapes, and these angels persevered in faith, worship, humility, and serene subordination to Allah. (Figure 13, p. 50)

Functions of Major Angels:

Four of the most known angels are: Jibraeel (Gabriel), Mikaeel (Michael), Izraeel, and Israfeel. Gabriel delivers Allah's Commands to His Prophets. Michael distributes sustenance to mankind. Izraeel, also known as the Angel of Death, takes out the soul from human beings. Israfeel will blow a trumpet on the Final Day, a Day which will cause death to every living thing, and then he will blow the trumpet a second time in which all the dead will be resurrected and be taken for Judgment.

Prophet Mohammad received revelation through the vision of the Angel Gabriel, who patiently persevered to teach Prophet Mohammad the Qur'an. Angels are sent to bring revelation to Allah's messengers and to execute Allah's Decrees:

"He doth send down His angels with inspiration of His Command, to such of His servants as He pleaseth (saying): 'Warn (man) that there is no Allah but I: so do your duty unto Me.'" (Qur'an 16:2)

While angels are sent down to inspire prophets, they will also descend in ranks once this world ends:

"The Day the heaven shall be rent asunder with clouds, and angels shall be sent down descending (in ranks) - that Day, the dominion as of right and truth, shall be (wholly) for Allah Most Merciful: it will be a Day of dire difficulty for the disbelievers." (Qur'an 25:25-26)

It is beyond our greatest imagination to conceive how the heavens would burst asunder. Nonetheless, we must be patient and certain that, by the Glory of Allah, it will take place. And who are the purest and noblest of Allah's creation - none other than the angels who are infinite in their praise and glory for Allah. All the power of angels is derived from Allah. In the end, man will have attained the highest spiritual level and may even have more power and position than angels in Paradise. We are reminded here that angels bowed down to Adam.

Man's Earthly Deeds are Recorded by Angels:

Attaining the highest spiritual level does not come automatically. While in existence in this ephemeral or transient world, man must prove himself worthy of this level. Angels are sent to protect man and to record his deeds - good and bad:

"Behold, two (guardian angels) appointed to learn (his doings) learn (and note them), one sitting on the right and one on the left. Not a word does he utter but there is a sentinel by him ready (to note it)." (Qur'an 50:17)

The angel on the right notes the good deeds; the angel on the left records the bad deeds. Note the sabr (endurance) of these angels who persist throughout the life of a person just to record his deeds.

Angel's Duties to Allah:

Angels never tire in their praise to Allah:

"Their hearts are filled with the fear of Allah. Their backs are bent from long prayers to Him. Their fervent desire for Him makes them persist in their prayer for His Favor. Their relative proximity only makes them more ardent in their subordination to Him. Their long and zealous prayers never give rise to conceit. Their serene subordination to Him entice them to belittle their deeds. They never feel the passage of time in their adoration of Allah. Their yearning for Him never weakens. Their tongues never cease praising Allah. They are never distracted from voicing His Praise. They invariably obey His Orders and never rest or relax in their prayers. They are not concerned with worldly desires or prone to laziness." (al-Imam Ali)

Here we note that angels symbolize the ultimate essence of sabr. Their prayers are perpetual and they endure forever in complete worship and praise for Allah. Man, in this world, conditions himself to sabr through prayer. How well he demonstrates his faith in prayer and other noble deeds will determine his position in the Hereafter. While man's prayers, for example, occupy only a short time in his daily activities in this world, his prayers in the Hereafter are continuous as demonstrated by the angels. For, like the angels, it is in the persistence of man's obedience and worship that he attains the highest glorification of Allah.

And we are reminded by the angels of our responsibility to Allah:

"(The angels say:) 'We descend not but by command of thy Lord: to Him belongeth what is before us and what is behind us and what is between: and thy Lord never doth forget. Lord of the heavens and of the earth, and of all that is between them: so worship Him, and be constant and patient in His worship: knowest thou of any who is worthy of the same Name as He?'" (Qur'an 19:64-65)

We must not be impatient. Allah does not forget. Our duty is to be consistently patient and to seek Allah's Blessing and Mercy.

Sabr and Prophets

"Not an apostle did We send before thee without this inspiration sent by Us to him: that there is no Allah but I; therefore, worship and serve Me." (Qur'an 21:25)

35

Sabr is notably exemplified in the lives of the Prophets (*Anbiya*). Extreme difficulty and obstacles faced the Prophets as they continued their quest to teach the people the way of Allah. But with patience and perseverance they succeeded:

"Patiently, then, persevere: for the promise of Allah is true: and ask forgiveness for thy fault, and celebrate the praises of thy Lord in the evening and in the morning." (Qur'an 40:55)

Need for Final Revelation:

Prophet Moses exercised patience and perseverance as did Prophet Jesus. Their disciples followed the true meaning of the Books. However, in the centuries to follow, Jews and Christians began to make revisions to the original Books and, as such, gave more reason for the Final Revelation sent to Prophet Mohammad.

Role of Prophets:

All the prophets had a role to perform. The summation of their spiritual works became fully realized with the Final Revelation - the Qur'an. Reward for those who followed these prophets and punishment for those who did not is clearly stated:

"Therefore, patiently persevere, as did (all) apostles of inflexible purpose; and be in no haste about the (unbelievers), on the Day that they see the (punishment) promised them, (it will be) as if they had not tarried more than an hour in a single day. (Thine But) to proclaim the Message: but shall any be destroyed except those who transgress?" (Qur'an 46:35)

Each of the five Major Prophets (Noah, Abraham, Moses, Jesus, and Mohammad) delivered the Message of Allah. These Prophets delivered to mankind the spiritual works by which we can perform good deeds. There are twenty-five (25) Prophets listed by name in the Qur'an of which five are Major Prophets. (Figure 14, p. 51)

However, there were many other prophets whose names were not cited in the Qur'an:

"We did aforetime send Apostles before thee: of them there are some whose story We have related to thee, and some whose story We have not related to thee...." (Qur'an 40:78)

Sabr and Resurrection

Resurrection (*Ma'ad*) is inevitable, and the Day of Judgment (*Yawm al-Qiyamah*) is ever so near:

"The Day when they will hear a (mighty) Blast in (very) truth: that will be the Day of Resurrection." (Qur'an 50:42)

Concept of Time and Space:

Time and space as we know it ends. A new life will begin. Our patience and perseverance in the previous life will now be rewarded. For those who did not pay heed to self-sacrifice and constancy will now pay the immeasurable price:

"The angels and the Ruh ascend unto Him in a Day the measure whereof is (as) fifty thousand years: Therefore do thou hold patience - a patience of beautiful (contentment). They see the (Day) indeed as a far-off (event): but We see it (quite) near." (Qur'an 70:4-7)

In this world, fifty thousand years seems a very long time. In the Hereafter, it may be equated to a mere moment. In this world, with all its misfortunes, we should be patient and have faith and trust in Allah. For us, resurrection may seem a very far-off event. However, the reality of resurrection is that it is so very near. The nearness becomes more profound when one realizes that he cannot go back to the previous life to correct his wrongs. He rests in his grave until summoned by Allah for his accountability. The end result for the winners is a Garden that awaits them as a Reward for their patience. For the transgressors, the Supreme Penalty of Hell awaits them:

"And have patience with what they say, and leave them with noble (dignity). And leave Me (alone to deal with) those in possession of the good things of life, who (yet) deny the truth; and bear with them for a little while. With Us are Fetters (to bind them) and a Fire (to burn them), and a Food that chokes, and a Penalty grievous." (Qur'an 73:10-13)

Instead of nourishing him, the sinner's food chokes him and the result is perpetual pain and suffering in Hell. Whereas in Heaven, the faithful are nourished with the blessings of Allah as a reward for their perseverance:

"What is with you must vanish: what is with Allah will endure. And We will certainly bestow, on those who patiently persevere, their reward according to the best of their actions. Whoever works righteousness, man or woman, and has faith, verily, to him will We give a new life, a life that is good and pure, and We will bestow on such their reward according to the best of their actions." (Qur'an 16:96-97)

The spiritual good that one performs in this temporal life will endure forever. With faith, one can accomplish the spiritual good and Allah will reward according to the best of our actions. In this world, every soul shall be given a body and the being will have the free will and volition to do as it pleases. On the Day of Resurrection, the being will have a complete manifestation as to the existence of Allah, and on that

Day each being will be summoned to witness their own actions on earth. The end result is reward or punishment for their earthly actions.

B. Branches of Faith

Sabr and Prayer

"For Him (alone) is prayer in Truth: ...for the prayer of those without Faith is nothing but (futile) wandering (in the mind). Whatever beings there are in the heavens and the earth do prostrate themselves to Allah...." (Qur'an 13:14-15)

Faith as Foundation: Prayer as Security:

Here, faith is a requisite for prayer. We are reminded that sabr is the requisite for faith. Faith alone is not enough. Faith and prayer are justified when we worship and submit to Allah alone. This is accomplished by being steadfast and patient.

To merely pray, for example, without steadfastness and self-restraint in your prayer weakens that person's resolve. Sabr becomes the essence of prayer. With sabr, one can pray the daily requirement of seventeen rikats and come away with more piety than one who lacks sabr and prays a thousand rikats daily. Habitual prayer, with patience, brings us closer to Allah. Through prayer, believers are able to express their faith in words:

"The believers must (eventually) win through...." (Qur'an 33:1)

Seven Jewels of Faith:

The winners are those who follow the "seven jewels" of faith. (Figure 15, p. 52) The "seven jewels" are:
1. Humility
2. Avoidance of vanity
3. Charity
4. Sexual purity
5. Fidelity to trusts
6. Observe covenants
7. Get closer to Allah

To practice these "seven jewels" is difficult but can be achieved through perseverance:

"Nay, seek (Allah's) help with patient perseverance and prayer: it is indeed hard, except to those who bring a lowly spirit, who bear in mind the certainty that they are to meet their Lord, and that they are to return to Him." (Qur'an 2:45-46)

Sabr: Guardian of Prayer:

The aforementioned verse instructs us to seek help through both sabr and prayer. The mental attitude one practices in prayer manifests itself in our daily activities. To seek help only through prayer falls far short of ensuring that we will behave accordingly in our daily activities. Sabr guards the dignity of the prayer and ensures that our behavior will reflect the true essence and meaning of prayer:

"O ye who believe! seek help with patient perseverance and prayer: for Allah is with those who patiently persevere." (Qur'an 2:153)

Here, Allah stresses the impact of patience by giving it more importance than prayer. So be thorough with your prayer and do not be hasty. Our spiritual well-being is enhanced through prayer:

"And establish regular prayers at the two ends of the day and at the approaches of the night: for those things that are good remove those that are evil: be that the word of remembrance to those who remember (their Lord). And be steadfast in patience; for verily Allah will not suffer the reward of the righteous to perish." (Qur'an 11:114-115)

Haste makes waste. Be patient and practice each of the five prayers. To start on the right path each day, pray the morning prayer (*fajr*) on time for it sets the stage for the rest of the day. With the morning prayer, we are reminded of our obligation and duty to Allah. We end the day with the early night prayer (*'isha*) by thanking Allah for His Blessing having watched over us by warding off evil and guiding us toward the good deeds.

Once each week we meet at a mosque to perform the Friday Prayer. This Friday gathering of Muslims at a mosque further strengthens their unity via steadfastness in their prayer. At that Friday gathering, one can readily see how patient the Muslims are as they stand side by side, in unity, as they prostrate in prayer. Even at the prayer during the pilgrimage, notice how patiently the millions of Muslims stand in prayer. It is patience that makes the unity prayer or individual prayer a success.

Daily Prayers:

There are five daily prayers, which are obligatory and incumbent upon every Muslim to observe and perform:

1. Dawn prayer (*al-fajr*)   two parts
2. Noon prayer (*al-zuhr*)   four parts
3. Afternoon prayer (*al-'asr*)   four parts
4. Evening prayer (*al-maghrib*)   three parts
5. Night prayer (*al-'isha*)   four parts

The total number of parts (*rikats*) in the five prayers combined is seventeen. In addition to these daily prayers, there are several other prayers, among which are the prayer for the dead and the holiday prayers.

We must be active in our search for truth through prayer. With patience one can reach a higher level of understanding in his prayer, thereby setting him on the path of truth as he confronts the tumultuous world which is full of discord and disenchantment.

Sabr and Fasting

Fasting (*siyam*) is referred to as self-restraint (sabr):

"O ye who believe! Fasting is prescribed to you as it was prescribed to those before you, that ye may (learn) self-restraint." (Qur'an 2:183)

Fasting means to abstain primarily from eating, drinking, smoking, and sex from dawn to sunset. Ramadan, according to Prophet Mohammad, is:

"....a month of endurance (sabr), and the reward for endurance is Paradise....a month in which a believer's provisions are increased."

Ramadan:

It is incumbent upon Muslims to fast during the month of Ramadan, the ninth month of the Islamic lunar calendar. Muslims, for example, who are sick, traveling, or frail due to old age are exempt from fasting. However, missed fasts must be done at another time when the Muslim restores his health or completes his travel. There are penalties for violating an obligatory fast. The type of violation will determine the extent of the penalty.

There are other recommended fasts outside the month of Ramadan, such as the fast during the first and third days of the month Muharram, the months of Rajab and Sha'ban, and the first and last Thursday of every lunar month, just to mention a few.

One of the ways to practice sabr during the month of Ramadan is to recite the entire Qur'an during that month. All Muslims, rich and poor, come into balance during Ramadan as all are equally engaging in the same type of abstention. During this month, the Muslim becomes healthier due to a balance in the diet, a more balanced character due to self-restraint, and a reward from Allah for abstention and submission. Sabr permeates both aspects of self-denial and repentance. (Figure 16, p. 53)

Self-Denial:

The principle of self-denial by fasting is not new. As Muslims, we differ in the way we fast from those who preceded us; we differ in the number of days we fast as well as the time and manner of fasting. Self-restraint here is in the manifestation of piety (*taqwah*). Not only do we control our natural physical desires but we also abstain from satisfying our carnal desires. With piety we can achieve self-restraint (sabr). Ramadan is the month in which the fast is practiced:

"Ramadan is the (month) in which we sent down the Qur'an, as a guide to mankind, also clear (Signs) for guidance and judgment (between right and wrong). So everyone of you who is present (at his home) during that month should spend it in fasting...." (Qur'an 2:185)

During the month of Ramadan, we practice sabr in our fast and reflect upon the words of Allah by reciting verses from the Qur'an, the Book sent to mankind during this holy month. We guard against our temptations and frailties of character by offering ourselves in deep meditation as we cement our metaphysical relationship with Allah. Fasting and prayer are the means by which this is accomplished as we struggle (*jihad*) in our quest for unity.

There are many passions, carnal desires, and temptations which threaten the dignity of man. How we thwart off these weaknesses is through fasting. It is fasting which increases our resolve and self-restraint, resulting in patience and perseverance against evil. Fasting becomes our struggle and resistance against evil, and with prayer we are guided to the straight path of purity:

"Say: 'O my servants who have transgressed against their souls! Despair not of the Mercy of Allah: for Allah forgives all sins: for He is Oft-Forgiving, Most Merciful. Turn ye to your Lord (in repentance) and bow to His (Will) before the Penalty comes on you: after that ye shall not be helped....'" (Qur'an 39:53-54)

Repentance:

Repent and work righteousness before it becomes too late:

"He is the One that accepts repentance from His servants and forgives sins: and He knows all that ye do." (Qur'an 42:25)

Do not put off repenting until tomorrow for tomorrow may never come as you may find yourself resting in your grave awaiting the Final Judgment. Reforming oneself immediately is true repentance:

"Every disease has a cure and the cure of the sins is repentance." (Prophet Mohammad)

41

Prophet Mohammad is instructing us to repent for our sins. Repentance reassures one's faith and increases that person's resolve. It is patience that makes repentance a realization, since it gives the proper direction for the soul to adjust and reform. Fasting places the repenter in a controlled self-environment, and because of this it plays a far more effective role in the liberation of man from the bondage of sinful acts.

Here, the linkage between fasting and repentance leads one to achieve piety by way of patience. True repentance is achieved when a person feels ashamed of what he has done and is willing to reform. Prophet Mohammad had made a speech during the month of Ramadan where he states that Ramadan is the best of all months, its days the best of all days, its nights the best of all nights, and its hours the best of all hours. He reminds the Muslims to pray, read the Qur'an, refrain from what Allah forbids, repent, and ask for Allah's Forgiveness.

Regarding who are the good people, Prophet Mohammad said:

"Those who feel happy when they do something good. If they commit a sin, they ask for pardon and repent. If anyone renders them any service, they are thankful to him. If they are afflicted by a distress, they endure it with patience. If they are annoyed with anyone, they forgive him."

To repent for a sin means that one's faith is sound, since that person can still distinguish between right and wrong. Fasting during the month of Ramadan is not just self-restraint of food, water, and sex during the prohibited portion of the day but also self-restraint at all times against some of our weaknesses: backbiting, slandering, gambling, and alcohol consumption. Here, fasting becomes fully attained as we achieve our major struggle against ourselves.

Sabr and Alms

Alms (*Zakat*):

Zakat is an Islamic tax which must be paid on certain kinds of products (for example, produce and livestock) and on gold and silver. *Zakat* may be given to the needy and poor; religious leaders; non-Muslims attracted towards Islam; travelers experiencing hardship; Muslims having difficulty repaying debts; or on anything considered in the way of Allah. Additionally, we are required to pay one-fifth (*khums*) of surplus income.

Charity (*Sadaka*):

Charitable deeds are of value when they are done without any self-serving motive. *Sadaka* (charity) for our relatives, the orphans, the poor (especially those who do not ask for charity), and other people or institutions in need are the responsibility of each and every Muslim. Alms and charity are complementary and are often considered the same. Al-Imam Ali said:

"Fortune is not stable; one day it smiles at you, the next day it will frown upon you. Do not exult if it is a good day, and be patient if it is a grim one."

Practice alms and charity as often as you can. While charity is usually associated with monetary gestures, it can be fulfilled with non-monetary considerations. The importance of al-Imam Ali's maxim is that it warns us that while we may be on "top of the world" with wealth and fortune, we could wake up the next day in hardship and even poverty. Do not frown upon the one who receives charity as you may one day be its recipient. Above all, practice patience whether in wealth or in poverty. Charity without patience will not last. Be charitable in whatever you give. Al-Imam Ali further said:

"Do not be shy when giving little; deprivation is still less."

Do not wait to fulfill the requirement of charity. The very little you give still means a great deal to the one who receives. Never underestimate the effect of a small contribution, for that mere gesture may be the spark which sustains the life of the needy. Be spontaneous in your generosity. That spontaneity which comes from patience, humbles the giver and enlightens the receiver. You feel good and your spirit is cleansed because your patience in giving was ample reward for the good you performed. The good deed resulting from charity endures and lasts as long as the giver maintains his silence. Be habitual in charity, and do not seek a purpose for doing it. Do not give charity for the purpose of getting back more than what was given, for surely you will lose the reward and your efforts will be in vain.

According to al-Imam Ali, the Prophet Mohammad had said:

"Preserve your faith with charity; protect your money with zakat; and ward off calamities by praying faithfully to Allah."

The giver of charity practices patience in his giving, and the receiver of charity practices patience in his receiving. Allah grants the giver patience as he reflects on the needy. At the same time, Allah grants the receiver patience as he reflects on his need:

"Persist in your action with a noble end in mind. Be straightforward, and stick to endurance and piety." (al-Imam Ali)

Sabr and Pilgrimage

"And complete the Hajj or 'umra in the service of Allah...."
(Qur'an 2:196)

The complete pilgrimage (*hajj*) is performed during the first ten days of the month of *zul-hajj* (last month of the Islamic calendar), while a less formal pilgrimage (*'umra*) is performed at any time of the year. The complete pilgrimage is obligatory on every Muslim once in their lifetime as long as they fulfill the conditions of age, health, sanity, and affordability. In addition, if there are travel restrictions to Mecca or if the area of Mecca is unsafe due to war, for example, then there is no obligation to perform the pilgrimage at that time. Should future conditions change for the better, then the Muslim, if able, should perform the pilgrimage.

Meaning of Pilgrimage:

Pilgrimage is a place and time when one expresses his gratitude to Allah for His blessings through submission to Him. Muslims from all over the world gather together in unity and in humility to purify their faith through prayer. They seek to cleanse themselves of their worldly weaknesses which inhibit their steadfastness and self-sacrifice to Allah.

At the pilgrimage, they have the opportunity to express their solemn sacrifice to Allah and to ask for His Forgiveness and Guidance in order to perfect themselves as Muslims; thus they will be better able to serve Islam. What the pilgrimage teaches us is to strive and fight in defense of truth, a struggle which first comes from within oneself. This test of self-sacrifice (sabr) continues after the pilgrimage where the person is expected to practice Islam in all its beauty and manifestations.

By sharing food with other fellow Muslims during the pilgrimage, particularly, the sacrifice of meat which is eaten for food and distributed to the poor and needy, one becomes truly thankful of Allah, the Sustainer:

"To every people did We appoint rites (of sacrifice), that they might celebrate the name of Allah over the sustenance He gave them....Allah is One Allah: submit then your wills to Him (in Islam): and give thou the good news to those who humble themselves. To those whose hearts, when Allah is mentioned, are filled with fear, who show patient perseverance over their afflictions, keep up regular prayer, and spend (in charity) out of what We have bestowed upon them." (Qur'an 22:34-35)

Here we are instructed to take our trials with patient perseverance and not to be afraid of the afflictions of this mortal life. Pilgrimage is a form of worship (*ibada*) which covers all aspects of human life. It trains Muslims to sacrifice all their wealth, time, and energies in the way of Allah. The course to follow is the straight path, and to follow that path with faith, good deeds, truth, and constancy (sabr).

Ritual:

Muslims go to Mecca and perform circumambulation (*tawaf*) around the Holy Shrine (*Ka'bah*). Whether in nice weather or inclement weather, Muslims perform this ritual with love and devotion. During the pilgrimage, Muslims visit many holy shrines in Mecca and Medina. These visits leave an everlasting impression in the minds and hearts of the Muslims, and they pray to achieve tranquillity (*sakina*) to increase their faith.

There is no distinction between race, color, sex, rank, or nationality as all are equal, and each has the opportunity to express their gratitude and love for Allah. This annual gathering brings Muslims from all over the world closer together and closer to Allah. How they become closer is through their perseverance (sabr).

Sabr and Struggle

In Islam, there are two forms of *jihad* (major and minor). The *minor jihad* (struggle) is a two-fold concept in Islam which means to (a) defend Islam against all aggressors; and (b) to enjoin good by prohibiting evil.

Concept of Sacrifice (Struggle):

Jihad essentially means the endeavor towards sacrifice or struggle for the sake of Allah. Self-sacrifice, another aspect of sabr, may require fighting in Allah's cause. Here, sabr becomes the spirit of jihad. To serve Allah is the cause, and worldly possessions and motives dissipate.

Defense is an aspect of jihad for the cause of righteousness and justice. Defending Islam by way of physical activity against the oppressor is one aspect of jihad, while scholarly work, charity, or a contribution of some sort are other aspects. Jihad is not always physical; quite the contrary, it is primarily non-physical and the self-sacrifice one makes may be in terms of wealth, property, or forgiveness. For example, to reconcile differences with each other is at the pinnacle of jihad.

Those who wish to destroy Islam must be encountered:

"And if ye do catch them out, catch them out no worse than they catch you out: but if ye show patience, that is indeed the best (course) for those who are patient. And do thou be patient, for thy patience is but from

Allah; nor grieve over them: and distress not thyself because of their plots." (Qur'an 16:126-127)

Man in his struggle is often confronted with opposition. Disputes or fights may result. A Muslim who is struck a blow is entitled to return a similar blow to his attacker. With jihad one reaches sabr by turning the other cheek, restraining himself, and sets an example of the highest form of conduct and behavior. He walks away from the dispute or fight; or he tries to console his adversary with kind words or gestures. With sabr he will find the way to resolve the conflict peacefully.

Allah protects the patient ones no matter how distressful a situation may be.

Struggle Against Egoism (*Major Jihad*):

A wife who is faithful to her husband and, likewise, a husband who is faithful to his wife is yet another aspect of jihad. Each has a duty as a spouse, and the fulfillment of that duty is the forbearance or sabr they have for each other. Each must set aside their own egos and work towards a unified marriage:

"...They are your garments and ye are their garments...." (Qur'an 2:187)

Here, jihad against egoism is the *major jihad*, a jihad of self-restraint. (Figure 17, p. 54) To fight against one's own wild passions and egoistic pleasures is the best jihad. Men and women are each other's garments and as such have mutual interaction in terms of support, comfort, and protection. Garment (*libas*) symbolizes the mutual relationship of husband and wife. Each spouse develops an Islamic personality, a personality in which consciousness, love, and fear of Allah predominates. This Islamic personality results in a jihad against egoism and those elements within the self which are at opposition to fulfilling this personality.

FIGURE 10

THE BEAUTIFUL NAMES OF ALLAH

1.	The Beneficent	34.	The All-Forgiving	67.	The One
2.	The Merciful	35.	The Appreciative	68.	The Eternal
3.	The Sovereign	36.	The Most High	69.	The Able
4.	The Holy	37.	The Most Great	70.	The Powerful
5.	The Source of Peace	38.	The Preserver	71.	The Expediter
6.	The Trusted	39.	The Maintainer	72.	The Delayer
7.	The Protector	40.	The Reckoner	73.	The First
8.	The Mighty	41.	The Sublime One	74.	The Last
9.	The Compeller	42.	The Generous One	75.	The Manifest
10.	The Majestic	43.	The Watchful	76.	The Hidden
11.	The Creator	44.	The Responsive	77.	The Governor
12.	The Evolver	45.	The All-Embracing	78.	The Most Exalted
13.	The Fashioner	46.	The Wise	79.	The Source of All Goodness
14.	The Forgiver	47.	The Loving	80.	The Acceptor of Repentance
15.	The Subduer	48.	The Glorious One	81.	The Avenger
16.	The Bestower	49.	The Resurrector	82.	The Pardoner
17.	The Provider	50.	The Witness	83.	The Compassionate
18.	The Opener	51.	The Truth	84.	The Eternal Owner of Sovereignty
19.	The All-Knowing	52.	The Trustee	85.	The Lord of Glory and Bounty
20.	The Constrictor	53.	The Most Strong	86.	The Equitable
21.	The Expander	54.	The Firm One	87.	The Gatherer
22.	The Abaser	55.	The Guardian	88.	The Self-Sufficient
23.	The Exalter	56.	The Praiseworthy	89.	The Enricher
24.	The Honorer	57.	The Counter	90.	The Preventer
25.	The Dishonorer	58.	The Orignator	91.	The Distresser
26.	The All-Hearing	59.	The Restorer	92.	The Propitious
27.	The All-Seeing	60.	The Giver of Life	93.	The Light
28.	The Judge	61.	The Bringer of Death	94.	The Guide
29.	The Just	62.	The Living	95.	The Incomparable
30.	The Kind	63.	The Self-Subsisting	96.	The Everlasting
31.	The Aware	64.	The Finder	97.	The Supreme Inheritor
32.	The Forebearing One	65.	The Noble	98.	The Guide to the Right Path
33.	The Great One	66.	The Unique	99.	The Patient

47

FIGURE 11

DEVOTION TO ALLAH

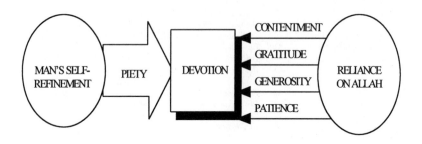

SOURCE: TALLAL ALIE TURFE

FIGURE 12

BOOKS OF ALLAH

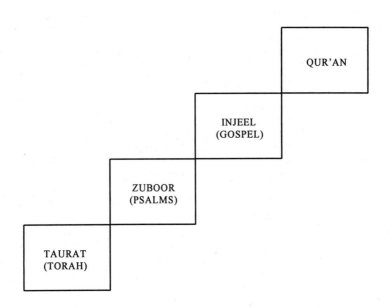

SOURCE: QUR'AN 3:3; 4:163

FIGURE 13

DESCRIPTION OF ANGELS

- Perseverance (sabr) in faith, worship, humility
- Serene subordination to Allah
- Some remain only prostrating, some bowing, some standing
- Aspire to obedience and glorification of Allah
- Never rest or relax in prayers
- Yearning for Allah never weakens
- Never cease nor distracted from praising Allah
- Treasure mercy of Allah
- Hearts filled with Allah's knowledge and sincere love
- Hearts filled with fear of Allah
- Do not perceive Allah in any form, shape or image
- Nor see Allah as contained
- Some convey Allah's revelation to messengers
- Some speak to prophets
- Some carry out Allah's orders and injunctions
- Some charged with the protection of Allah's creatures
- Some guard the gates of Heaven
- Some have their feet deep in the earth and heads up in the skies
- Eyes never sleep
- Minds never roam aloof
- Bodies never weaken nor fatigue
- Memories never falter
- Minds free from personal concern or worry
- Have wings
- Bodies not confined to space
- Shoulders are cushions of Allah's throne
- Different shapes
- Different levels of power
- Never ascribe or claim participation in creation
- Not constrained by guilt or sin
- Not affected by eventualities of the passage of days and nights
- Never dispute among themselves
- Some are transparent as clouds
- Some are great as mountains
- Some are obscure as night
- Not concerned with worldly desires or prone to laziness
- Previous deeds are nothing in their eyes
- Satan has no influence on them
- Not divided by envy, suspicion or vanity
- Do not stoop to folly
- Never distracted by bias, weakness, desire or temptation

SOURCE: DERIVED FROM AL-IMAM ALI'S NAHJUL BALAGAH

FIGURE 14

PROPHETS

- 1. ADAM
- 2. IDRIS
- 3. NOAH*****
- 4. HUD
- 5. SALIH
- 6. ABRAHAM*****
- 7. LOT
- 8. ISHMAEL
- 9. ISAAC
- 10. JACOB
- 11. JOSEPH
- 12. JOB
- 13. SHU'AIB
- 14. MOSES*****
- 15. AARON
- 16. DAVID
- 17. SOLOMON
- 18. ELIAS
- 19. ELISHA
- 20. ZUL-KIFL
- 21. JONAH
- 22. ZACHARIAH
- 23. JOHN
- 24. JESUS*****
- 25. MOHAMMAD*****

*****MAJOR PROPHETS

SOURCE: QUR'AN 2:30-31; 6:83-86; 7:73; 7:85; 7:158; 11:50; 21:85

FIGURE 15

SEVEN JEWELS OF FAITH

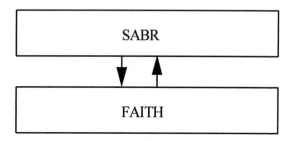

- •Humility
- •Avoidance of Vanity
- •Charity
- •Sexual Purity
- •Fidelity to Trusts
- •Observe Covenants
- •Get Gloser to Allah

SOURCE: QUR'AN 23:1-11

FIGURE 16

FASTING

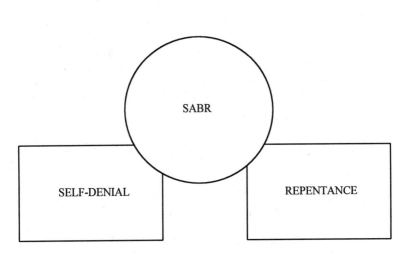

SABR

SELF-DENIAL

REPENTANCE

SOURCE: TALLAL ALIE TURFE

FIGURE 17

STRUGGLE

MAJOR STRUGGLE	MINOR STRUGGLE
• STRUGGLE AGAINST EGOISM	• DEFEND ISLAM • ENJOIN GOOD • PROHIBIT EVIL

SOURCE: TALLAL ALIE TURFE (DERIVED FROM QUR'AN)

PART III: JURISPRUDENCE OF SABR

Sabr and Islamic Law

Al-Imam Ali said:

"Patience is not only in the face of what you do not like, but also of what you like."

Basically, there are at least five kinds of sabr (patience) in relation to Islamic law. (Figure 18, p. 59)

Duty (*Wajib*):

Reference here is to our moral obligations:

"O ye who believe! Fulfill (all) obligations." (Qur'an 5:1)

Basically, duty is comprised of three levels of obligations: divine obligations (duty to Allah), mutual obligations (duty to ourselves), and tacit obligations (duty to others). All three obligations are sacred whether divine, mutual, or tacit. To fulfill these obligations, one must be in total concert with his intention, that is disciplining oneself towards achieving the Mercy of Allah. In this worldly existence we cannot isolate these three duties - they are interrelated and must be practiced in consonance with each other:

1. Duty to Allah: We must strive in the way of Allah and seek His Mercy through piety (*taqwah*). Not only must we be cognizant of Allah but we must worship Allah as well. To obey and serve Allah is our major duty to Him:

"And obey Allah and His Apostle; and fall into no disputes, lest ye lose heart and your power depart; and be patient and persevering: for Allah is with those who patiently persevere." (Qur'an 8:46)

2. Duty to Ourselves: How we fulfill the duty to ourselves (personal obligations) is through refinement of our souls (*tazkiya*). Unless we know ourselves we will never reach self-refinement. With self-refinement we attain prosperity (*falah*). Prophet Mohammad said:

"Whoever knows himself knows Allah."

Spiritual well-being is the order of the duty we have towards ourselves. While we seek self-refinement of our soul, we must also ensure the best in our mental health and physical health. We have a responsibility to ourselves. We must practice patience and refrain from the bad things in life: illegal use of drugs, prostitution, and other vices which not only endanger man's body but his soul as well.

3. Duty to Others: Here we have a duty to our spouse, family, children, relatives, friends, neighbors, co-workers, classmates, the needy, orphans, and many other people (social obligations) with whom we come into contact whether daily or occasionally:

"By no means shall ye attain righteousness unless ye give (freely) of that which ye love; and whatever ye give, of a truth Allah knoweth it well." (Qur'an 3:92)

The ultimate test of charity is seen here - to give up something we value greatly. What one gives up may be his property, possessions, or just a small token or gesture of kindness. The greatest gift one can give is his personal time - to be patient and make time to help the poor, the needy, and orphans as well as time to teach one's children the religion of Islam.

Forbidden (*Haram*):

Islam is the path of moderation, not extremes. Everything is not prohibited nor is everything allowed. It is a balance. The list of prohibitions is small in reality. That is because most things are *halal* (allowable), for example, all types of meat are *halal* except for a couple of types like pork.

There is a code of ethics and morality that we must follow, and this requires us to strive towards overcoming our weaknesses. Only through our perseverance and firmness in determination can we truly overcome these weaknesses.

Desirable (*Mustahabb*):

Be steadfast (sabr) in doing things which are desirable. For example, in addition to the regular format for prayer, we may also add to the prayer for Allah to forgive us and to watch over our deceased. This is a form of *mustahabb* which is not only desirable but recommended. We may perform supplication (*du'a*), additional prayers, which are not mandatory but recommended.

Reprehensible (*Makruh*):

This refers to those practices which are undesirable and which should be avoided if possible. For example, becoming wealthy is good; however, do not be jubilant to the point that the thought of wealth controls your attitude and behavior:

"Fortune is not stable; one day it smiles to you, the next it will frown upon you. Do not exult if it is a good day, and be patient if it is a grim one." (al-Imam Ali)

Again we see where patience is the panacea or solution to this unwarranted exultation. Similarly, performing good deeds is a great feat in Islam. However, that good deed may become nullified if the performer brags about it:

"A good deed that endures is better than many which do not last." (al-Imam Ali)

Here, too, we see sabr (endurance) as the key to sustaining one's good deed. It is undesirable for one to boast about his good deed or to make someone feel obligated to you for having performed that good deed. Again al-Imam Ali gives us the cure:

"Tolerance is a protective cover; wisdom is a sharp sword. Cover your deficiencies with tolerance and fight your passion with wisdom."

Allowable (*Mubah*):

What is permitted is *halal*. We must be patient in understanding what is allowable and what is not. There are guidelines toward this end. However, it is best to consult with a religious leader for specifics on interpretation of Qur'anic verses and *hadith* (traditions).

Just to cite one example where mubah applies. In the case of prayer, there are conditions permissible where one can recite his prayer (*salat*). The place should be one which is stationary, and the direction of the prayer should be towards the *qiblah* (towards Mecca). *Mubah* dictates how we are to perform our prayer, particularly, in places that may be impure (*najis*). Here, the positioning of the forehead on the floor should be done with extreme precaution so as to not invalidate the prayer.

Sabr: A Dichotomy

As previously stated, we have sabr with both the fortunate times and the unfortunate times. Practicing sabr while we are wealthy or while we are poor is not easy. To be moderate in your lifestyle when wealthy may be hard to accomplish as it is difficult to be hopeful when in the face of poverty. The dichotomy of sabr permeates the continuum of extreme polar opposites: "good times" versus "bad times." (Figure 19, p. 60)

It is not easy to practice sabr when you are miserable and in the doldrums or when you face calamity and cruelty. Likewise when you are happy you should be moderate in your jubliant behavior.

With wealth and good fortune one should practice moderation and charity:

57

"Woe to every (kind of) scandal-monger and backbiter, who pileth up wealth and layeth it by, thinking that his wealth would make him last forever!" (Qur'an 104:1-3)

Being poor requires patience at its ultimate test. Poverty is extremely difficult to deal with, especially when it reaches the level of malnutrition or starvation and ultimately death, the latter which may be a blessing to relieve the person from his misery.

Similarly, a person afflicted with a disease may suffer long years of pain and suffering. If healthy, a person should always remember that he is not immune to sickness.

Sometimes a marriage fails to succeed and the end result is divorce, the latter which may be a blessing in disguise. A marriage relationship requires the utmost in commitment and fidelity between the spouses, and sabr is the key towards cementing this bond. However, if there is disloyalty between the two spouses or a situation that is totally unbearable, then divorce may be the only recourse. While divorce leaves one with an emotional breakdown, that person must turn to sabr for strength to weather the storm and to readjust to society:

"If a wife fears cruelty or desertion on her husband's part, there is no blame on them if they arrange an amicable settlement between themselves; and such settlement is best; even though men's souls are swayed by greed. But if ye do good and practice self-restraint, Allah is well-acquainted with all that ye do." (Qur'an 4:128)

FIGURE 18

SABR IN RELATION TO ISLAMIC LAW

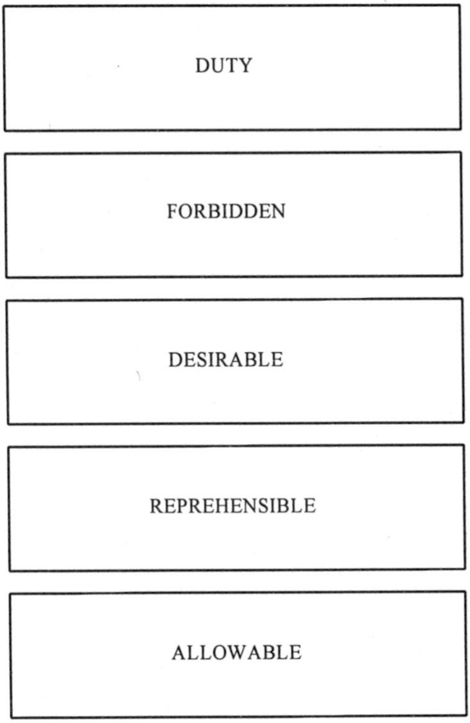

DUTY

FORBIDDEN

DESIRABLE

REPREHENSIBLE

ALLOWABLE

SOURCE: ISLAMIC SHARI'AH

FIGURE 19

SABR: A DICHOTOMY

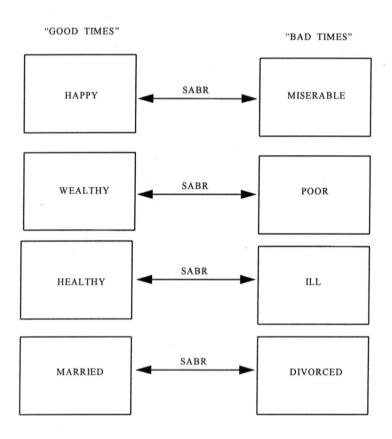

"GOOD TIMES"

"BAD TIMES"

SOURCE: TALLAL ALIE TURFE

PART IV: PHILOSOPHY OF SABR

Elements of Human Existence

Basically, there are four elements of human existence: (1) physical elements; (2) elements of the senses; (3) power elements; and (4) spiritual elements. These elements intertwine with the body (prime matter) and soul (substantial form).

Sabr and Blessing

Among the many blessings (*ni'ma*) from Allah are life and death:

"And they returned with Grace and Bounty from Allah: no harm ever touched them: for they followed the good pleasure of Allah: and Allah is the Lord of bounties unbounded." (Qur'an 3:174)

Physical sustenance is a blessing. Allah provides us with light and rain as well as food and the sense of sound, sight, taste, smell, and touch. Moral sustenance, likewise, is a blessing. Allah provided us with prophets to teach us spiritual well-being and the concepts of Islam. These blessings should not be taken for granted or abused. We need to practice self-restraint (sabr) relative to these blessings. We must be grateful to Allah for bestowing upon us such favors. Life is from Allah and death is from Allah:

"It is He who created death and life." (Qur'an 67:2)

Allah's Blessing transcends the concepts of life, death, partition (*barzagh*), resurrection, and eternity. (Figure 20, p. 68)

Life and Death

"Death is the door to eternity, while living is the key to death." (Tallal Alie Turfe)

Depending on how one chooses to utilize the blessings of Allah in the physical life will determine what lies beyond the door - heaven or hell. Peace will be for those who lived a good life, while punishment awaits those who lived a bad life. Man is an everlasting being, and death is only a step towards this eternal life. This eternal future rests on the deeds and actions of one's stay in the earthly existence.

Islam provides us with certain goals and objectives in our earthly life, and we must adopt these principles and follow them. These goals and objectives are blessings from Allah. Man has the free will, yet another blessing, to choose his path in life. How well he chooses decides his outcome. Man must strive for perfection, even though he knows that he may never reach it. Yet his attempt towards perfection and self-realization (*idrak an-nafs*) in sabr (endurance) will be looked upon by Allah most favorably.

Partition, Resurrection and Eternity:

This partition (*barzagh*) is the place after death but before the Day of Judgment. Death is the separation of the soul from the physical body. That soul travels to a partition (*barzagh*) in which it becomes more aware of the facts of existence. The partition lies between the present life and the resurrection. In the resurrection every soul shall be given a visible body. Now everyone becomes perfectly aware of the existence of Allah. On the Day of Judgment the earthly actions (good deeds and bad deeds) of everyone will be unfolded in their presence. It is only those who patiently persevered in the previous life who will reach happiness in the Eternal Garden.

According to the Qur'an, life after death is a second creation. Birth and rebirth are blessings (*ni'ma*) from Allah. The human hope to transcend death is not the hope to escape death, but the hope of the resurrection. At the resurrection, human beings will be given a new body to participate in the new creation. This is possible since Allah knows every type of creation. Existence is dependent on the Will of Allah. Birth and rebirth are two distinct blessings (*ni'ma*) of a first and second creation. The resurrection of the body is not in any way conditioned upon the immortality of the soul. Both body and soul are dependent on the creative Will of Allah.

So let us not lose sight of the meaning of the term "blessing." The actions performed by Allah are indeed blessings:

"...And if you count Allah's Favors, you will not be able to number them...." (Qur'an 14:34)

All the perfections of this earth and the universe are favors from Allah.

Human Soul

The Qur'an tells us not only that human beings are a unity of body and soul, but also that there is another element in them other than the soul which is different from the body. That element we note in the Qur'an is the term *nafs* (its plurals are *anfus* and *nufus*). *Nafs* refers both to the individual self and to the human soul. When it refers to the human soul, the Qur'an characterizes it as *ammarah* (Qur'an 12:53), *lawwamah* (Qur'an 75:2), or *mutma'innah* (Qur'an 89:27):

62

"'Nor do I absolve my own self (of blame): the (human) soul is certainly prone to evil, unless my Lord do bestow His Mercy: but surely my Lord is Oft-Forgiving, Most Merciful.'" (Qur'an 12:53)

"And I do call to witness the self-reproaching spirit: (eschew evil)." (Qur'an 75:2)

"(To the righteous soul will be said:) 'O (thou) soul, in (complete) rest and satisfaction!'" (Qur'an 89:27)

- **Evil Soul (*Ammarah*):** This is the soul that inclines us to evil. The mind of man is ever ready to incite to evil. This means that the human self urges man towards undesirable and evil ways as it is opposed to his attainment of moral perfection. At this stage, man is at the opposite end of sabr.

- **Conscious Soul (*Lawwamah*):** This is the soul that constantly upbraids itself in the quest for goodness. This reproving self or self-reproaching spirit is the second source of human state for which the moral state is generated. It reproves man on vice and is not reconciled to man's submitting to his natural desires. It desires that man should be in a good state and should practice good morals. As it reproves every vicious movement, it is called the reproving self. Here, man is conscious of sabr as he strives to achieve it. The self seeks to comprehend within itself high moral qualities and is disgusted with disobedience but cannot achieve complete success.

- **Tranquil Soul (*Mutma'innah*):** This is the tranquil soul of the virtuous believer that will return to Allah. This is the stage when the soul of a person being delivered from all weaknesses is filled with spiritual powers and establishes a relationship with Allah. Here, sabr is achieved with complete success.

Sabr and Elements of Human Existence

The physical elements are comprised of earth, air, fire, and water. The elements of the senses are sight, sound, touch, taste and smell. The power elements consist of the intellect, anger, passion, and imagination. The spiritual elements are faith, prayer, fasting, charity, pilgrimage, struggle, ethics, and beliefs. (Figure 21, p. 69) Sabr interacts with these elements as it is the origin of the power elements and the spiritual elements.

Concepts of Creation and Moral Qualities:

Khalq means creation. *Khulq* means moral qualities and not natural impulses. To every physical action there is an inner quality which is moral. For instance, a person shedding tears through his eyes is a physical action, while the inner or moral quality is what we call tenderness. Likewise, a person defends himself against the attack of an enemy with his hands, and corresponding to this physical action there is an inner or moral quality called bravery. Sometimes a person does not wish to attack one who attacks him and forbears to take physical action against a wrongdoer. Here, the corresponding inner or moral quality is called forbearance or endurance:

"And thou (standest) on an exalted standard of character." *(Qur'an 68:4)*

This means that all high inner or moral qualities such as benevolence, courage, justice, mercy, and sincerity were combined in the person of the Prophet Mohammad. All the natural qualities of man such as courtesy, modesty, integrity, steadfastness, chastity, piety, bravery, generosity, forbearance, and endurance, when under the guidance of reason, are characteristics of inner or moral qualities.

Sabr: A Prescription for Purification

It is in the arena of the power elements that we now focus our attention. We need a prescription or remedy in order to turn our weaknesses (deficiency or excessiveness) into strengths (moderation). Deficiency or excessiveness occurs when we are not in control of the powers of our human soul. These powers are: (1) power of intellect; (2) power of anger; (3) power of passion; and (4) power of imagination. The prescription for turning these weaknesses into strengths is sabr. For it is sabr that is the origin of these powers and the well of the soul. (Figure 22, p. 70)

- **Power of Intellect:** How the power of intellect is utilized determines its deficiency or excessiveness. For example, the absence of mind, logic, and reason is the source of ignorance, whereas their presence is the source of wisdom. Turning the deficiency of ignorance into the moderation of wisdom is done by way of sabr. Sabr is related to the strength of our intellect. The origin of the human mind is the intellect. The origin of the intellect is sabr. Here sabr links with the Islamic concept of cleanliness, the latter which cleanses and purifies the inner soul so that the individual reaches the level of the peaceful and pure heart as well as mind. The more intellectual one becomes the wiser and stronger that person becomes, and the better equipped that person is to overcome any adverse emotion. The bad emotion results in a loss of realistic thought thereby minimizing one's intellect. This bad emotion can emanate from a deficiency in the power of intellect (ignorance) or the excessive use of the power of intellect (slyness). The end result is that the person succumbs to

64

the level of ignorance or slyness by becoming emotionally unstable, that is, the person passes the limit of reasonable thinking.

People often face problems, particularly, in times of sickness and adversity. People face these problems from various standpoints. The losers are those who are ignorant and sly and do not know how to deal with the problems; while the winners are those who are patient and know how to deal with the problems wisely.

- Powers of Anger, Passion, and Imagination: Likewise, cowardice can be overcome with courage (power of anger), laziness can be overcome with chastity (power of passion), and prejudice can be overcome with justice (power of imagination). Cowardice and impatience are vices of deficiency in relation to courage and patience, respectively. The relevant vices of excess would be a reckless bravado and a sort of witless passivity in the midst of avoidable suffering and hardship. We think of courage as the paramount virtue of self-restraint. Indeed we are more than a little tempted to speak of it as the only virtue of self-restraint. This grossly underestimates the importance of patience.

The moral failures of war may be those without the patience to survive great anger as well as those without the courage to resist great fear. Patience can ensure compliance among the victims of exploitation, such as the poor. Consider the affinity between patience and the idea of giving oneself to the good. If we are to construe our relation to the good as a matter of service, we must learn that the despair or anger we might experience in bearing the burdens of service are to be resisted as emotions that threaten to alienate us from the good. By allowing such emotions to engage our thoughts and actions, we cease to give ourselves to the good. The more we assume that the hardships or evils we experience can be set right with enough justice or courage the less room there is for the reasonableness of a moral posture that counsels acceptance of the limits of our capacity to make the good we crave our own.

Courage derives from steadfastness. To be steadfast against every personal passion or against any calamity that attacks like an enemy and not to run away out of cowardice is true courage. Thus, there is a great difference between human courage and the courage of a wild beast. A wild animal is moved only in one direction when it is roused, but a man who possesses true courage chooses confrontation or non-resistance whichever might be appropriate to the occasion.

There are many examples of how sabr can be the vehicle for purifying these four powers of the human soul. The examples chosen, however, provide a clear picture and understanding as to why people lose control of their inner selves because they lack the quality of sabr and cleanliness. It is very important to purify ourselves with sabr so that our soul will be cleansed of evil and corruption, and that we will thus be guided by ethical and moral virtues. Only in this way can we prepare ourselves to receive the unlimited devotion of Allah. Here, our struggle (jihad) is for perpetual purification. The straight path guides us towards the goal of perfection in Islam.

With justice, we reach the highest level of the power of imagination. For justice is the origin of all ethical virtues. It is the faculty of justice which illuminates all of the four powers of the human soul. It is the faculty of justice which guides us as individuals or as a society:

"We sent aforetime Our Messengers with Clear Signs and sent down with them the Book and the Balance of Right and Wrong, that men may stand forth in Justice; and We sent down Iron, in which is (material for) mighty war, as well as many benefits for mankind, that Allah may test who it is that will help, unseen, Him and His Messengers; for Allah is Full of Strength, Exalted in Might (and able to enforce His Will)." (Qur'an 57:25)

The three gifts from Allah are the Book, the Balance, and Iron which stand as symbols of the three things which hold a society together. Justice is the means by which each person receives his due.

As individuals, justice is our metaphysical relationship with Allah. Here, our actions in this world will determine our reward or punishment in the Hereafter. Individual justice means that we should refrain from committing sins. When we reach this level of purification through sabr we will have attained the level of becoming just ('adil).

We also have social justice, that is, the justice of honoring the social rights of others within a society or community. We should not trespass upon the rights of others. Establish justice and goodness in a society. The prophets endeavored to establish piety in the lives of individuals in order that truth and justice should prevail in any society.

Finally, there is the justice which requires us to remember our loved ones who had passed away. How we remember our dead is by practicing ethical virtues such as kindness and charity. And it is sabr which provides us with the prescription towards achieving this end.

Regarding sabr, there are three warnings: (1) do not be lazy and give up hope but, rather, face trouble with strength; (2) do not fall into boredom; and (3) do not blame Allah whatsoever. The patient ones are the knowledgeable ones who have the knowledge of reality. Prophet Mohammad asked his people what level they have reached in their faith.

They answered by saying patience during adversity, thanking Allah for their wealth, and to accept that which is beyond their control. Prophet Mohammad responded by telling them that they are the wise and learned.

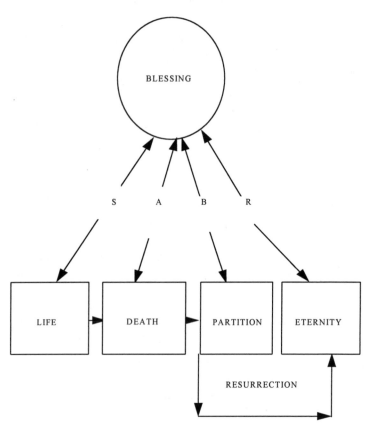

FIGURE 20

SABR AND BLESSING

SOURCE: TALLAL ALIE TURFE

FIGURE 21

ELEMENTS OF HUMAN EXISTENCE
(INTERACTION OF SABR)

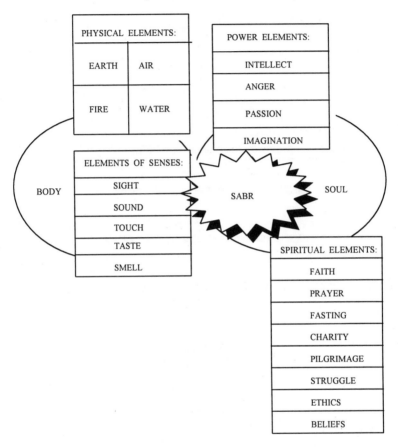

SOURCE: TALLAL ALIE TURFE

69

FIGURE 22

SABR: A PRESCRIPTION FOR PURIFICATION

SOURCE OF POWER	DEFICIENCY	MODERATION (SABR)	EXCESSIVENESS
•INTELLECT	Ignorance	Wisdom	Slyness
•ANGER	Cowardice	Courage	Recklessness
•PASSION	Laziness	Chastity	Voraciousness
•IMAGINATION	Prejudice	Justice	Tyranny

SOURCE: TALLAL ALIE TURFE

PART V: SOCIAL PSYCHOLOGY OF SABR

Sabr and Enlightenment

The interaction of sabr and enlightenment (*enarat*) radiates the highest level of spiritual attainment that one can achieve. The Qur'an specifically relates to the "Book of Enlightenment" (*Kitab-al-Munir*) which literally refers to a fundamental guide to conduct:

> *"Then if they reject thee, so were rejected apostles before thee, who came with Clear Signs, Books of dark prophecies, and the Book of Enlightenment." (Qur'an 3:184)*

Munir means "to enlighten" while *enarat* more closely relates to the term "enlightenment."

However, we must be very careful not to confuse the Islamic enlightenment with the Age of Enlightenment that prevailed in the Eighteenth Century.

Age of Enlightenment (Anti-Islam):

The Age of Enlightenment during the Eighteenth Century was applied to the often radical philosophy of the age, particularly to England, France, Germany, and Italy. European writers challenged theology, and they used critical reasoning to free minds from prejudices, unexamined authority, and oppression by church or state. Characterized by a questioning of tradition and a growing trend toward individualism, empiricism, and attempts to scientific reasoning, the movement developed many ramifications - religious, political, scientific, moral, and even aesthetic. Committed to free men's minds from the oppression of dogma and authority was the challenge undertaken by atheists and deists in particular. Man's right to direct his own destiny insofar as he was able was asserted even when a vague belief in the power of a guiding deity was retained. The Christian church was under severe attack, and the religion of Christianity was being severely threatened.

Enlightenment Defined from Islam's Perspective:

Enlightenment for Muslims takes a different path. In Islam, we are suppose to question and use our faculties of reason in order to find absolute truth. There is no blind following or imitation. One must always question his values to make sure they are in accordance with the Divine Law as stated in the Qur'an. It is impossible for reason to extend beyond the boundaries of Islam, because there is no contradiction between reason and Islam. On the contrary, reason of the mind leads one to the path of Islam. As Muslims, we are encouraged to seek knowledge from the cradle to the grave. Before Islam, man was to limit himself and his mind. When

71

faced with a contradiction in dogma, he was told to follow the law strictly by faith and negate reason. This imprisoned man's soul. Islam opened the gate to reason, stating that all knowledge and truth emanates from Allah; therefore, an unbiased search for truth and knowledge leads one directly to the path of Islam. The eighteenth century "Age of Enlightenment" was a backlash to religious restraints on correct reasoning. Islam does not place a boundary. Islam is the epitome of reason. It is Allah who is the giver of enlightenment. To be enlightened in Islam means to gain spiritual insight and knowledge in the search for truth, understanding, and wisdom. This search takes on a commitment in one's mind, and it can only come about through one's endurance and patience. The religion of Islam gives us a realistic perspective of enlightenment. This allows man to better understand himself while at the same time liberating himself from ignorance and confusion. Therefore, man is now able to restore his self-dignity and self-identity.

Cowardice and impatience are vices of deficiency in relation to courage and patience. Let us look at the example of a man who grows blind in the prime of his life. There is nothing that can bring back his sight. The potential for a good life, however, remains. He is healthy, prosperous, and surrounded by the people who love him. However, he is fearful of how others will regard him now that he is blind. He always pitied the blind, and the thought of being a pathetic spectacle to others is terrifying. His fear of humiliation makes him hide from the world. Although others reassure him that independence and competence can be regained with effort and flexibility on his part, he doubts his own capacity to learn a new way of life. Trying and failing to learn is more frightening than failing by not trying at all, and so he drifts helplessly.

In this example, this blind man has no patience for the moral task his blindness has set him, and no amount of courage or fortitude can compensate for the absence of that virtue. Enlightenment by way of patience is what he needs because it entails a discipline of those particular emotions that threaten to loosen or destroy one's hold on the good in circumstances of this kind. In courage, there is discipline of the fear that would make us cowards and the overweening confidence that would make us reckless. In patience, anger and despair are the things to be controlled if we are to cleave to the good against the temptations of impatience or a dejected passivity.

Sabr and enlightenment interact through the virtues of truth, understanding, knowledge, and wisdom. This interaction is further strengthened by one's self-concept, self-esteem, and self-fulfillment. (Figure 23, p. 85)

72

Self-Concept:

The self-concept has a powerful influence on one's behavior, perhaps, the most powerful influence. Man has a basic tendency to strive, actualize, maintain, and enhance himself:

"Man gets only what he strives for." (Qur'an 53:39)

The person develops this self-concept in order to gain confidence and feel good about himself or herself. There are boundaries which one must not extend beyond. The danger of enhancing one's self-concept outside the parameters of Islam, for example, an egotist, miser, gambler, drunkard, to mention just a few, renders that person a failure in his faith. Therefore, man's self-concept is one which strives toward the goal of patience and perfection in Islam, and one of the ways this is achieved is by performing good deeds:

"As for those who strive for Our cause, We will definitely guide them to Our paths." (Qur'an 29:69)

Self-Esteem:

Controlling self-esteem helps shape and mold one's self-concept. Developing positive self-esteem means to regard life and its surroundings with respect and affection. We become more positive about our feelings for ourselves. As our opinion of ourselves improves, we become better Muslims as well. People with high self-esteem take risks, and each risk they take teaches them something. Risk, however, requires patience.

Self-esteem is an extremely powerful factor in our growth and development as Muslims. To grow Islamically, we must practice endurance. Part of that endurance and power comes from its uniqueness. It operates as a mechanism for maintaining our inner consistency. It helps determine how our experiences are interpreted. It provides a set of expectancies - what we do in situations and how we interpret what others do in situations.

Self-Fulfillment:

Becoming the best we can as Muslims requires a commitment and the patience to succeed. We need to be committed towards working up to our potential to learn and understand the concepts of Islam. This results in self-fulfillment or self-satisfaction. Knowledge and understanding give direction for one to realize his objectives and goals, while wisdom enhances one's self-fulfillment to its fullest potential:

"For Allah has sent down to you the Book and Wisdom and taught you what you knew not." (Qur'an 4:113)

And truth is the light which enlightens one's mind and keeps him on the straight path. When self-fulfillment comes into balance with the self-concept the end result is self-esteem, the ultimate in happiness. Just as man needs to come into balance with his society, so does self-fulfillment need to come into balance with the self-concept. The way to achieve this balance is by way of self-esteem, the basis of which is intellectual enlightenment and the zenith of which is sabr. This balance gives the person an integrated self, a higher standard of perfection. What emanates from this integration is the value of truth. And this truth allows one to fulfill his submission to Allah. Those who accept the guidance of truth will purify their minds and bodies:

"Say, O you men! Now Truth has come to you from Your Lord! Those who receive Guidance do so for the good of their own souls; those who stray do so to their own loss." (Qur'an 10:108)

Criteria for Developing Islamic Self

When we come to learn and understand this balance, we gain an entirely new perspective about ourselves. So how can we create, nurture, and then effectively use this perspective to help us be what we want to be - better Muslims?

- **Be Patient:** Self-discovery, self-development, self-awareness, self-esteem, and self-confidence take time to acquire. One thing you can do is to try giving away yourself. Instead of pulling everything toward yourself, allow things to go out from you. When you make important connections with others through your commitments, attention, time, respect, and attitudes toward them, you will be defining yourself by what you are giving to them - by what you are giving away. Patience will help you be what you want to be because you can do anything you want if you stick to it long enough. But, remember, patience is not passive; on the contrary it is active; it is concentrated strength.

- **Be Purposeful:** Have a goal; have a set of goals. Plan and have alternative plans as well. But be true to yourself. What you do while in the process of becoming not only can influence what you become, but it can provide a clearer definition of the perspective that you seek. So plan your work and work your plan because the person who fails to plan, plans to fail!

- **Be Persistent:** Stick with your perspective. In today's society, we want instant gratification. Why? Because everything appears to be instant - instant coffee, instant potatoes, instant winners, and instant rewards. Self-fulfillment through one's perspective is not instant. Becoming the me we want to be is not instant. The only thing about it that is instant is when we can start. We cannot do everything at once; but we can do something at once!

Enlightenment and the Cosmos

Controlling the Islamic self is not an easy task. It requires control of one's inner thoughts and actions. Becoming enlightened in Islam is that which is accompanied by understanding one's self-concept, controlling his self-esteem, and attaining self-fulfillment by way of patience, purposefulness, and persistence. Control is achieved by way of order and harmony within the self. The cosmos (*nitham*) is not only the systematic order and harmony within the universe, but also within a society, institution, family, and above all within one's self.

Islamic Personality and Islamic Morality

One of the ways in which we can achieve the tranquil soul is by developing an Islamic personality:

"Therefore, be patient with what they say and celebrate (constantly) the praises of the Lord, before the rising of the sun, and before its setting; yea, celebrate them for part of the hours of the night and at the sides of the day: that thou mayest have (spiritual) joy." (Qur'an 20:130)

Evil hovers around us. We must be patient and ask Allah for guidance so that we can avoid evil. The Islamic personality makes the believer cherish his human dignity and prestige and accept his responsibilities as a Muslim. And what better example of the Islamic personality than that of Prophet Mohammad.

The justification of religious morality, that is, Islamic morality promises the continuance of life in the Hereafter for the morally good individuals. In Islam, there is no distinction between theoretical morality and physical morality. Morality deals with determining right from wrong. Morality is comprised of virtues. Faith, righteous deeds, truth, and patience are the basic virtues of Islamic morality. Man gains eternal happiness through moral virtues. The Prophet Mohammad had said:

"My religion is based on cleanliness."

Cleanliness here does not just refer to our daily washing and cleansing of our bodies. There is a higher meaning to this *hadith* (tradition), a meaning which attaches itself to the inner purity of the soul. We must cleanse our thoughts and our hearts in order to attain ultimate and final perfection. In striving towards perfection through self-purification, Allah will guide us:

75

"And those who strive in Our (Cause) - We will certainly guide them to Our Paths: for verily Allah is with those who do right." (Qur'an 29:69)

And the path is the straight path (*sirat al-mustakim*). We must free ourselves from the spider's web of this frail world. We must walk the path of struggle against immoral tendencies. All that we can do is to strive in the way of Allah. With firmness of purpose, determination, and patience we can attain the Mercy of Allah.

Revolving Hierarchy of Islamic Personality and Morality:

As a guideline, the Revolving Hierarchy of Islamic Personality and Morality begins with faith (*iman*) and ends with endurance (sabr) and then proceeds back to faith. (Figure 24, p. 86) Tantamount to this circular effect is the analogy of proceeding from theory to fact and then back to theory again.

As you can see, the Revolving Hierarchy is composed of six groups:

1. Self-foundation (*asas an-nafs*)
2. Self-security (*aman an-nafs*)
3. Self-awareness (*waee an-nafs*)
4. Self-achievement (*tahkeek an-nafs*)
5. Self-satisfaction (*retha an-nafs*)
6. Self-realization (*idrak an-nafs*)

With faith as the self-foundation, we proceed upward until we attain self-realization by way of endurance (sabr), and then we proceed back to faith. We always need to reinforce and strengthen our Islamic personality and morality by absorbing ourselves in these criteria.

Having faith leads us to practice at least the five requirements of prayer, fasting, alms, pilgrimage, and struggle. With this we become aware of truth as we seek knowledge, understanding, and wisdom. The straight path via worship and piety results in the self-achievement of righteous deeds, prosperity, and action. Therefore, as part of our prayer we say, "Come to prayer; come to prosperity; come to action."

Prosperity or salvation (*falah*) occurs when man has freed himself from selfishness and basic desires. Prosperity emanates from man's self-achievement. One who purifies himself through worship and is humble and patient will attain prosperity and success:

"But those will prosper who purify themselves, and glorify the name of their Guardian Lord, and (lift their hearts) in prayer." (Qur'an 87:14-15)

76

"O ye who believe! Persevere in patience and constancy; vie in such perseverance; strengthen each other; and fear Allah; that ye may prosper." *(Qur'an 3:200)*

Tranquillity and happiness are the levels of self-satisfaction arising from self-achievement. At the zenith of the fulfillment of these needs is self-realization through endurance. Similarly, moving from endurance downward through each of the six categories makes us more cognizant of our role as Muslims and of our contribution towards Islam.

Moral judgment is applied to all activities of man, which results in a single undivided Islamic personality. Through prayer, we can strengthen our Islamic personality and resolve in order to grapple with evil and overcome its dastardly venom. Struggle *(jihad)* manifests itself in prayer:

"Enjoin prayer on thy people, and be constant therein. We ask thee not to provide sustenance: We provide it for thee. But the (fruit of) the Hereafter is for righteousness." *(Qur'an 20:132)*

True, Allah provides sustenance for all, just and unjust, in this ephemeral world, but this is a transient existence which ends almost as soon as it begins. So be prudent and wise in how you utilize that sustenance, and exercise your sabr and struggle *(jihad)* in the way of Allah by doing good and prohibiting evil:

"So persevere in patience; for the promise of Allah is true: and whether We show thee (in this life) some part of what We promise them, - or We take thy soul (to Our mercy) (before that), - (in any case) it is to Us that they shall (all) return." *(Qur'an 40:77)*

Justice will prevail. Every soul must return to Allah for His Justice and Judgment. Life in this world is very short; however, life in the Hereafter is eternal. Allah provides sustenance to the righteous in the Hereafter. The unjust are doomed to a dark and ghastly world of punishment.

Sabr and Comfort

"It is He Who sent down Tranquillity into the hearts of the Believers, that they may add Faith to their Faith; for to Allah belong the Forces of the heavens and the earth; and Allah is full of Knowledge and Wisdom." *(Qur'an 48:4)*

Comfort and Tranquillity:

Allah provides us with tranquillity *(sakina)* With a peaceful heart, tranquillity becomes the foundation for comfort *(salwan)*. Comfort is a practice we use often in our daily lives. To practice comfort independent of patience (sabr) renders its meaning and effectiveness to mediocrity. However, when combining it with sabr, we now have a fuller meaning and understanding. For example, to comfort one in her time of bereavement without sabr, falls far short of being effective. Just to say, "my deepest sympathy for the loss of your loved one" may merely catch the ear of the bereaved and dissipate very quickly. However, to empathize, that is, to feel what the bereaved feels, and then to comfort her has much more effect and meaning. It places you in the position of the bereaved as if you had suffered the loss as well. This is where patience, tranquillity, and comfort reach their highest point.

Have you noticed at times of funerals, when the bereaved family hover themselves around the deceased and submit themselves to prayer and supplication? They become totally oblivious to the surroundings and people around them. They are in a state of patience and comfort reflecting on the deceased only and reciting verses from the Holy Qur'an and echoing supplication. Others may be crying and screaming which do not help the deceased; rather, they detract from the concentration of those who offer their prayer and supplication.

Or take another situation when friends visit the family of the deceased at their home. Upon entering the house, the bereaved family offers you complete hospitality. They also begin to comfort you, perhaps, with expressions to put you at ease, or to utter words of praise to you, or to ask Allah to watch over your own deceased. Assume the bereaved had lost a son, nonetheless, praises someone else's children who are still living. This is the highest level of *salwan*, when the bereaved is comforting the visitors and friends even though it is he who had suffered the immediate loss. This we call *sabr wa salwan* (patience and comfort). Here, the bereaved had exercised self-restraint of his own emotions and with patience and constancy began to empathize with his friends by comforting them, perhaps, with a kind expression, an embrace, or a smile.

Take a mother who embraces her newly-born child. She comforts her child with all the love and affection she can render. She keeps a close vigil over her child. She weeps when her child takes ill. She rejoices when her child is healthy and strong. These are comforting signs coupled with her endurance to protect her child.

A parent that grows old and takes ill. The children rise up to their obligation and responsibility by nursing their parent by exhibiting kindness. By watching over their parent even if it means to provide a place in their home. While this type of care may take years as the children watch their parent suffer, the children never lose sight of their duty. With perseverance the comfort reaches its highest level of meaning.

Comfort is also the hallmark of a sound and successful marriage. Here, the test of sabr is when one spouse exercises patience in the face of the other spouse's bad temper. This high level of sabr is needed in order for the spouses to communicate more effectively with one another and to solidify their marriage. Prophet Mohammad had stated:

"Whomever is patient on his wife's bad attitude will be looked upon favorably by Allah just as was the case of Prophet Ayoub (Job)."

Comfort and Emotion:

One of the most difficult aspects of our lives is when we fall victim to an emotion (*enfial*) that is out of control. The panacea for controlling our emotions is to comfort (*salwan*) both our inner self and outer self. This comforting is accompanied by patience (sabr). (Figure 25, p. 87)

Emotion is defined as a strong, relatively uncontrolled feeling that affects our behavior. All of us experience a wide array of emotions. Emotions are generally triggered by environmental events and by physiological changes. Another characteristic feature of an emotional experience is cognitive thought. Emotions generally, though not necessarily, are accompanied by thinking. The types of thoughts and our ability to think "rationally" vary with the type and degree of emotion. Emotions also have associated behaviors. While the behaviors vary across individuals, and within individuals across time and situations, there are unique behaviors characteristically associated with different emotions.

Finally, and most importantly, emotions involve subjective feelings. In fact, it is the feeling component we generally refer to when we think of emotions. Grief, joy, anger, jealousy, and fear feel very differently to us. These subjectively determined feelings are the essence of emotion.

These feelings have a specific component that we label as the emotion, such as sad or happy. While emotions are generally evaluated (liked or disliked) in a consistent manner across individuals, and within individuals over time, there is some individual and situational variation. For example, few of us generally want to be sad or afraid yet we occasionally enjoy a movie or book that scares or saddens us.

One of the elements of ethics is conscience. When the feeling is based on the laws of reason, it leads one to the truth. For example, the concept of charity in Ramadan (*fitra*) emanates from one's conscience to perform a good deed. Not all personal feelings are ethical (for example, the feelings a mother has for her baby; it is what the natural law demands, Allah's laws, conscience and *fitra*).

A person's ethical beliefs or actions will be influenced by the personality traits of that individual. Emotions play a major role in how that personality unfolds. At times, a person's emotions are such that his personality exhibits a "double standard" as to what is perceived as acceptable behavior and what is believed to be, for example, acceptable Islamic practices. One who gambles at a race track or casino to acquire fortune may be an acceptable behavioral practice in some cultures, but it is definitely against Islamic law. Here, a great deal of effort is needed in order to control one's emotions.

The greater the amount of patience, the more willing one will be to invest time and effort towards projecting a favorable image of himself. Lack of knowledge and understanding of the proper conduct for the Islamic personality will lead the person into disarray thereby subjecting him to emotional instability such as fraud, deception, anger, and hate. Islam teaches us to guard against anger and wrath by remaining patient:

"...And those who restrain (their) anger and pardon men...." (Qur'an 3:134)

People need patience as a moral virtue to keep their lives in perspective. When people are anxious, they display a lack of patience and a deficiency in faith and hope. Impatience manifests itself in unreasonable anger, complaints, depression, and discouragement. Moreover, it prevents people from seeing the joy of loving and serving Allah. Impatience is also accompanied by insensibility, which ostensibly leaves people unmoved by human suffering, and a shutting off from the happiness that often arises from painful trials. During difficult times, people must remember that Allah has assigned a purpose to each life. Patience can aid people in the bouts with loneliness and anger that they will inevitably experience at various times in their lives.

Sabr (patience) is of at least three forms:
1. Patience during adversity and calamity
2. Patience in obedience to Allah
3. Patience in refraining from sin

If one has control of his emotions in the face of adversity or calamity, then this is sabr. If he becomes courageous during the battle, whether in time of war or the struggle (jihad) within one's inner self, then this is also sabr. When one wants to utter something which troubles his inner self but withholds that emotion by not uttering it or passing it on to others, then this, too, is an example of sabr.

To be patient relative to Allah's Obedience is far easier than to be patient relative to Allah's Punishment. One is in need of patience

80

during adversity, poverty, sickness, war, and so forth. Without sabr, one cannot survive these hardships. Control of one's emotions by way of sabr is the solution towards achieving Allah's Obedience.

Guarding against one's adverse emotions by exercising self-restraint is the surest way to prohibit evil and protect one from committing sins. All these forms of sabr are great examples of patience.

Regarding sabr, al-Imam Ali had stated:

"Sabr means two kinds of sabr: sabr with adversity and, more importantly, sabr on the things which Allah prohibits you from doing."

Selected Virtues Requiring Sabr

Forbearance (sabr) is the protector of tranquillity (*sakina*). Through tranquillity one can extol the virtues of courage (*shaja'a*), chastity (*'iffah*), gentleness (*hilm*), and abstinence (*zuhd*) to mention just a few. (Figure 26, p. 88)

Here we can see how sabr in these virtues poses a test for us:

"Be sure We shall test you with something of fear and hunger, some loss in goods or lives or the fruits (of your toil), but give glad tidings to those who patiently persevere, who say, when afflicted with calamity: 'To Allah we belong, and to Him is our return....'" (Qur'an 2:155-157)

Courage:

This term in itself is a definition of resolution and perseverance (sabr). With mental or moral strength to persevere, one proceeds withstanding fear, danger, and difficulty. With firmness of mind and will, one faces danger with all his fortitude and resilience. On the field of battle, one perseveres in his duty, for example, to defend Islam:

"...And David slew Goliath; and Allah gave him power and wisdom and taught him whatever (else) he willed...." (Qur'an 2:251)

Allah provided Prophet David with the courage to stand up against the giant, Goliath. Prophet David was victorious as he proved that courage overcomes fear, and it can withstand obstacles no matter how big or strong:

"When they advanced to meet Goliath and his forces, they prayed: 'Our Lord! Pour out constancy on us and make our steps firm: Help us against those that reject faith.'" (Qur'an 2:250)

We are reminded about the experiences of Prophet Moses and his brother, Prophet Aaron:

"Again (of old), We bestowed Our favor on Moses and Aaron, and We delivered them and their people from (their) Great Calamity; and

We helped them, so they overcame (their troubles)....." (Qur'an 37:114-118)

What greater courage could be demonstrated as they and their people persevered in the face of slavery and bondage in Egypt. The "Great Calamity" of not only slavery but also the desecration of their families, particularly, the killing of their male children by Pharaoh's army. Witness the courage of these people in the face of Pharaoh's threats:

"'Be sure I will cut off your hands and your feet on opposite sides, and I will cause you all to die on the cross.' They said: 'For us, we are but sent back unto our Lord: But thou dost wreak thy vengeance on us simply because we believed in the Signs of our Lord when they reached us! Our Lord! Pour out on us patience and constancy, and take our souls unto Thee as Muslims (who bow to Thy Will)!'" (Qur'an 7:124-126)

In all of history, none can match the courage of al-Imam Hussein (grandson of Prophet Mohammad) who, along with just over seventy of his companions, stood up to the tyrant, Yazid, and thousands of his soldiers in the battlefield at Karbala, Iraq. True, there were great feats of courage by prophets and other men and women; but in the instance of al-Imam Hussein the security of Islam was under siege. Al-Imam Hussein and his followers gave their lives to save Islam and, as such, won the battle.

Chastity:

This is the quality of being pure, modest, or decent. It requires, for example, that one refrain from acts of unlawful types of sexual intercourse, poor behavior and conduct, and immoral desires and lusts. Let us examine some historical examples of chastity as related to us in the Qur'an. To begin with, there is the example of Mary (Maryam), the mother of Prophet Jesus:

"And (remember) her who guarded her chastity: We breathed into her of Our Ruh, and We made her and her son a Sign for all peoples." (Qur'an 21:91)

Mary was the essence of chastity. Her chastity and the miraculous birth of her son, Prophet Jesus, were signs for everyone to know that Allah has the power over all things. Mary persevered (sabr) and remained pure for her entire life.

Chastity is just as important for men as it is for women. We recall the story of Prophet Joseph:

"But she in whose house he was, sought to seduce him from his (true) self....And (with passion) did she desire him, and he would have

desired her, but that he saw the evidence of his Lord: thus (did We order) that We might turn away from him (all) evil and shameful deeds: for he was one of Our servants, sincere and purified." (Qur'an 12:24)

The conflict here is that Prophet Joseph had already been purified but she was not. Not only did Prophet Joseph guard his chastity but he also respected his duty to the 'Aziz (Excellency) who had treated Prophet Joseph with the utmost respect and honor. Though temptation lurks in the midst, one must guard against it by putting their trust in Allah as did Prophet Joseph.

Gentleness:

This requires one's disposition to be mild and kind. In the state of anger, one acquires self-restraint through sabr, and as such exhibits the kindest of dispositions:

"It is part of the Mercy of Allah that thou dost deal gently with them. Wert thou severe or harsh-hearted, they would have broken away from about thee: so pass over (their faults), and ask for (Allah's) Forgiveness for them; and consult them in affairs (of moment). Then, when thou hast taken a decision, put thy trust in Allah. For Allah loves those who put their trust (in Him)." (Qur'an 3:159)

This verse is attributed to Prophet Mohammad, who, with his gentle disposition, was endeared to everyone. Even in the advent of disasters, such as the defeat at *Uhud* (major Islamic battle), we find Prophet Mohammad still exhibiting a gentle nature. The defeat at *Uhud* is a reminder of impatience; the Muslim scouts had left their positions before they were ordered to and, therefore, became vulnerable to attack. The lesson here is that when calamity strikes, be patient with kindness and gentleness in order to strengthen your resolve (sabr) and to weather the storm.

Kindness extends to all facets of life. In the case of parents, we should always lower our wing of humility and exhibit gentleness of the highest order:

"Thy Lord hath decreed that ye worship none but Him, and that ye be kind to parents. Whether one or both of them attain old age in thy life, say not to them a word of contempt, nor repel them, but address them in terms of honor. And out of kindness, lower to them the wing of humility and say: 'My Lord! Bestow on them Thy Mercy even as they cherished me in childhood.'" (Qur'an 17:23-24)

Worshipping Allah and being kind to parents are cemented together. We are pious in our worship to Allah, and we are also pious in our kindness to our parents. As parents were patient, gentle, and kind to

83

us when we were infants, they must now be afforded the same patience, gentleness, and kindness in their old age. In this regard, one must display the utmost in gentle humility in the treatment towards his parents.

With Prophet Jesus, Allah made him kind to his mother, Mary:

"(He) hath made me kind to my mother, and not overbearing or miserable...." (Qur'an 19:32)

Prophet Jesus was not overbearing. He practiced forbearance (sabr) in the relationship with his mother.

And how one treats his parents needs to comes from deep within, from the level of tranquillity and comfort coupled with patience. Always look to your parents with patience, gentleness, and kindness. Do not raise your voices above theirs. Extend your gratitude to them for they reared you when you were a child, became your friend when you were a teen, and became counsel to you when you attained adulthood.

Abstinence:

Refrain voluntarily from some action that is undesirable, for example, refrain from eating certain foods, drinking alcoholic beverages, or gambling. Abstention from extravagance, luxurious lifestyle, and forbidden pleasures and desires are still other examples. A forbidden pleasure may be cruelty or excessive punishment inflicted upon an enemy or transgressor. Yet another type of abstention is that against egoism and pragmatism. Still other aspects of abstinence are to refrain from backbiting, slander, jealousy, prejudice, materialism, tyranny, injustice, corruption, deception, fraud, hypocrisy, arrogance, and lying. The code of ethics for abstinence is detailed in the Qur'an and the Hadith (Traditions). To refrain from these weaknesses comes about through patience and the *major jihad* (struggle against the ego):

"Truly he succeeds that purifies it, and he fails that corrupts it!" (Qur'an 91:8-9)

Sabr: Self-Evaluation (Selected Criteria)

Each one of us should prepare a self-evaluation relative to how well we meet the criteria to reach and maintain sabr. (Figure 27, p. 89) While these criteria are not in any order of priority, they are significant and vital as they reinforce each other. For example, to be devout one must be actionable in prayer, or to be charitable one must be empathetic to the needs of the recipient. These criteria should be the minimum from which to build the Islamic personality.

FIGURE 23

SABR AND ENLIGHTENMENT

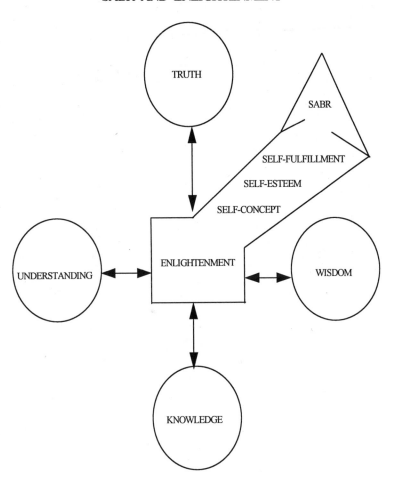

SOURCE: TALLAL ALIE TURFE

FIGURE 24

REVOLVING HIERARCHY OF ISLAMIC PERSONALITY AND MORALITY

SELF-REALIZATION   • Sabr

SELF-SATISFACTION
- Tranquillity
- Happiness

SELF-ACHIEVEMENT
- Action
- Prosperity
- Righteous Deeds
- Piety
- Worship
- Straight Path

SELF-AWARENESS
- Truth
- Wisdom
- Understanding
- Knowledge

SELF-SECURITY
- Struggle
- Pilgrimage
- Alms and Charity
- Fasting
- Prayer

SELF-FOUNDATION   • Faith

SOURCE: TALLAL ALIE TURFE

FIGURE 25

CONCEPT OF EMOTION

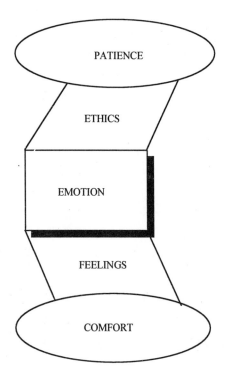

SOURCE: TALLAL ALIE TURFE

87

FIGURE 26

SELECTED VIRTUES REQUIRING SABR

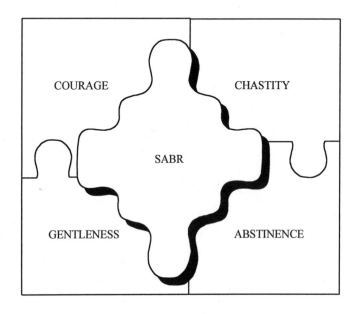

COURAGE

CHASTITY

SABR

GENTLENESS

ABSTINENCE

SOURCE: TALLAL ALIE TURFE

FIGURE 27

SABR: SELF-EVALUATION
(SELECTED CRITERIA)

Devout	Ethical	Honorable
Righteous	Courageous	Actionable
Truthful	Trustworthy	Chaste
Knowledgeable	Empathetic	Gentle
Understanding	Charitable	Hopeful
Prudent	Respectful	Humble
Just	Peaceful	Enlightened

SOURCE: TALLAL ALIE TURFE

PART VI: ROLE MODELS OF SABR: LIFE EXPERIENCES

Let us cite some examples of sabr as practiced by the minor prophets. Keeping in mind that the five major prophets (who received revelation from Allah and delivered Allah's Message) all practiced sabr, and their examples are very detailed in the Qur'an and the Hadith (Traditions).

Prophet Job (Ayoub)

A prosperous man who falls victim to misfortune holds steadfast (sabr) to his faith in Allah. Having lost his family, his servants, his cattle and property, his false friends, and becoming afflicted with physical maladies as well as losing his peace of mind, he humbles himself before Allah:

"And (remember) Job, when he cried to his Lord, 'Truly distress has seized me, but Thou art the Most Merciful of those that are merciful.' So We listened to him: We removed the distress that was on him, and We restored his people to him, and doubled their number - as a Grace from Ourselves, and a thing for commemoration, for all who serve Us." *(Qur'an 21:83-84)*

Prophet Job lived in Arabia about two thousand years before the birth of Prophet Mohammad. A very wealthy man, Prophet Job was constant in his prayer. What better example to test one's faith than to test one of Allah's most obedient worshippers. So perseverance (sabr) was put to the test. Suddenly, Prophet Job was struck with one calamity after another. His workers were killed and his cattle stolen. As he was being informed of this adversity, another calamity took place. A fire devastated his sheep and servants. And when he was being told of this calamity, another misfortune struck him. He lost all of his camels to a group of robbers. While he was being informed of this tragedy, he learns that all of his children as well as some other people were the fatal victims of a tornado which caused the roof to fall and crush them.

Through all these calamities never once did Prophet Job deter from his faith. He held his composure and humbled before Allah. More calamities hit him. He acquired a severe skin disease, perhaps, leprosy or lupus. His friends deserted him. Still he did not utter a word of complaint, and he maintained his sabr (steadfastness).

"O ye who believe! Seek help with patient perseverance and prayer: for Allah is with those who patiently persevere. And say not of those who are slain in the way of Allah: 'They are dead.' Nay, they are living, though ye perceive (it) not. Be sure We shall test you with

something of fear and hunger, some loss in goods or lives or the fruits (of your toil), but give glad tidings to those who patiently persevere, who say, when afflicted with calamity: 'To Allah we belong, and to Him is our return:' They are those on whom (descend) blessings from Allah, and Mercy, and they are the ones that receive guidance." (Qur'an 2:153-157)

Losing his wealth and property, his children, his workers, and developing a skin disease, all of these adversities did not break his spirit. What was so distressing to Prophet Job was that his friends had made false allegations against him. This was too much for him, so he broke down into tears. His friends made false allegations that he had received punishment from Allah for committing many sins. Prophet Job humbled himself in prayer and asked Allah to restore him back to health. Following his prayer, a revelation came to him from Allah:

"Strike the ground with your foot." (Qur'an 38:42)

Suddenly, a spring of water appeared from where Prophet Job struck his foot. He submerged himself into the water and became purified. Not only did he emerge from the water fully recovered, but he also looked younger and more handsome that even his wife could not recognize him. With this recovery, Allah also granted him with wealth and many children.

So Allah recalled to Prophet Job His Mercy and restored him with twice as much as he had before. Prophet Job had fought off evil with the best of weapons: humility, patience, and faith.

"...Truly We found him full of patience and constancy. How excellent in Our service! Ever did he turn to (Us)." (Qur'an 38:44)

Traditionally, Prophet Job has been regarded as an exemplary figure, principally of patience and forbearance, the pious virtue of restraining complaint or rebelliousness in deed, in word, or at times even in thought. But he is also taken actively as a paradigm of perfect charity, hospitality, and generosity and passively as a model recipient of divine grace and recompense. Prophet Job's story was inscribed as an example to all people, to teach them how to address adversity, intellectually as well as morally. The story of Prophet Job is intended to exemplify man at the extreme limits of endurance. The outcome of endurance is relief. He is an example for all mankind that there is no excuse for the neglect of Allah's worship. For none will have been more sorely afflicted than Prophet Job.

Prophets Ismail (Ishmael), Idris and Zul-kifl

These three prophets also practiced sabr:

"And (remember) Ismail, Idris, and Zul-kifl, all (men) of constancy and patience; We admitted them to our Mercy: for they were of the righteous ones." (Qur'an 21:85-86)

What a great example in Prophet Ismail, the "sacrifice to Allah," who held his resolve and guided his father, Prophet Abraham, to carry out his duty of sacrifice. The sacrifice was redeemed by the substitution of a ram under Allah's commands:

"Then, when (the son) reached (the age of) (serious) work with him, he said: 'O my son! I see in vision that I offer thee in sacrifice: now see what is thy view!' (The son) said: 'O my father! Do as thou art commanded: thou will find me, if Allah so wills one practicing patience and constancy!'" (Qur'an 37:102)

The quality of Prophet Ismail's constancy and patience is further exemplified and demonstrated in his prayer and charity:

"Also mention in the Book (the story of) Ismail: he was (strictly) true to what he promised, and he was an apostle (and) a prophet. He used to enjoin on his people prayer and charity, and he was most acceptable in the sight of his Lord." (Qur'an 19:54-55)

Prophet Ismail is described in the Qur'an as true to his promise. He was also referred by his people as the "the truthful." We note that the Qur'an alludes to him as one who is patient. His display of patience in persuading his father, Prophet Abraham, to carry out Allah's Command brings out the essence in one's faith.

Prophet Ismail, along with his father, Prophet Abraham, received Allah's commandment to rebuild the Ka'bah, the Sacred House of worship in Mecca. Prophet Ismail had twelve sons, one (Qidar) of which was the forefather of Prophet Mohammad.

Prophet Idris was also among those who patiently persevered:

"Also mention in the Book the case of Idris: he was a man of truth (and sincerity), (and) a prophet: and We raised him to a lofty station." (Qur'an 19:56-57)

Prophet Idris was in constant touch with his people, and he never shunned his responsibility to them. He steadfastly maintained his truth and sincerity in the highest station. We are reminded here that striving towards spiritual perfection should not deter a person from fulfilling his obligation to those whom he administers. In the case of Prophet Idris he achieved spiritual perfection, and he shared it with his people.

Prophet Idris was a very knowledgeable person, and he was called the "Learned Prophet," as he was the first man to write with a pen. His knowledge permeated throughout many disciplines, among which were the sciences, mathematics, and medicine. He was multi-lingual, and he had the ability to communicate in a native language. An advocate of the spiritual well-being of man, he constantly reminded the people that materialism was in conflict with religion, and that life on earth was of short duration. His patience, persistence, and perseverance were victorious over those who tried to deter him away from truth.

Prophet Zul-kifl also exhibited patience and perseverance in all its meaning. Chained and bound, he was unjustly tortured in prison rendering him dumb for a time. He maintained his patience in spite of the evils that plagued Israel during that time. He challenged the false leaders of Israel who exploited the people for their own selfish ends. Without any complaint, he withstood all calamities and hardships as he persevered in the fulfillment of his religious obligation.

Prophet David (Dawood)

Strength in courage and will was the hallmark of Prophet David's success:

"Have patience at what they say, and remember Our Servant David, the man of strength: for he ever turned (to Allah)." (Qur'an 38:17)

Prophet David had exceptional strength, both in body and mind. The Philistine army, guarded by their champion, Goliath, was at war with Israel. Saul (Talut) was the King of Israel who, along with his followers, asked for constancy in their fight against the Philistines:

"When they advanced to meet Goliath and his forces, they prayed: 'Our Lord! Pour out constancy on us and make our steps firm: help us against those who reject faith.'" (Qur'an 2:250)

Prophet David declined the armor and arms from King Saul, and approached the battle with Goliath with a sling and pebbles. With his steadfastness and determination, he unleashed his sling that knocked down Goliath. With Goliath's own sword, Prophet David slew him. The end result was total victory against the Philistines who were subdued.

Among the Books of Allah is the Psalms (*Zuboor*), which was revealed to Prophet David, whose voice was so magnificent that it penetrated the minds and hearts of his audience. In addition, he was able to communicate the Psalms and his thoughts to birds and animals as well.

93

What is the lesson we learn from the story of Prophet David? We learn that patience, determination, and courage will prevail over numbers, size, and strength. Power and wisdom derive from faith and truth. As with Prophet David, other Prophets (Noah, Abraham, Moses, Jesus, and Mohammad) patiently persevered in their struggle (*jihad*) to teach and perpetuate the faith of Islam.

Prophet Jacob (Yacoub)

With the machinations perpetrated against Joseph by his brothers when he was a boy, Joseph's father, Prophet Jacob, was confronted by his sons:

"They said: 'O our father! we went racing with one another, and left Joseph with our things; and the wolf devoured him but thou wilt never believe us even though we tell the truth.' They stained his shirt with false blood. He said: 'Nay, but your minds have made up a tale (that may pass) with you. (For me) patience is most fitting: against that which ye assert, it is Allah (alone) whose help can be sought.'" (Qur'an 12:17-18)

What magnificence in spiritual faith! Here Prophet Jacob is told that his son, Joseph, has been killed by a wolf. With firmness of heart and a steadfast mind, he knows it not to be true. It is that feeling that comes from the inner self which is full of righteousness and faith. A feeling which cannot be deterred or detracted from the truth. Prophet Jacob holds his heart and mind in patience and puts his faith in Allah.

Later, Joseph who had become a *wazir* (minister) of Egypt, and who had taken his brother Benjamin in his care, finally reveals himself to his brothers:

"They said: 'Art thou indeed Joseph?' He said, 'I am Joseph, and this is my brother: Allah has indeed been gracious to us (all): behold, he that is righteous and patient - never will Allah suffer the reward to be lost, of those who do right.'" (Qur'an 12:90)

The suffering endured by Joseph for many years now ends as he displays patience and empathy for the sake of his brothers. He instructs his brothers to take his shirt (symbolic of the falsified stained shirt which marked his disappearance) and cast it over the face of his father (Prophet Jacob) in order to see clearly.

So remember Allah at all times:

"Bear, then, with patience, all that they say, and celebrate the praises of thy Lord, before the rising of the sun and before (its) setting." (Qur'an 50:39)

94

And the best time to remember Allah is during prayer. Be steadfast and patient for Allah hears your prayer. Be guided by the teachings of our Prophets and do not go astray. When it came to prayer, Prophet Mohammad was very demanding:

> *"Having been promised Paradise, the Prophet, peace be upon him, was arduous in prayers, because Allah had ordered him, 'Enjoin prayers on your followers and persevere in offering them.' Therefore, he kept enjoining them on his followers and persevered in prayers."* (al-Imam Ali)

Imam Ali Zein al-Abideen

The son of al-Imam Hussein (grandson of Prophet Mohammad), al-Imam Ali Zein al-Abideen was born in 38 A.H. (658 A.D.) and lived for fifty-eight years. Following the martyrdom of his father, al-Imam Ali Zein al-Abideen served as Imam for thirty-four years. During all these years, he would be in constant prayer and supplication in remembrance of his father. He used to pray a thousand *rikats* (parts) during the day and the night, and he was popularly called *Sajjad* (one who prostrates).

When he used to perform ritual ablutions, the complexion of his skin would change. He was referred to as "the lord of the worshippers" *(abideen)*. One of his great characteristics is that he would restrain himself from anger in all situations. In the end he, too, was martyred.

It was al-Imam Ali Zein al-Abideen who continued the cause of Islam which his father had courageously died for. The Muslim world had to be reawakened to Islam, and it was al-Imam Ali Zein al-Abideen who successfully restored the Muslims back to the straight path. How he did this was by his example, and his example was prayer, the root essence of Islam. His numerous prayers and supplications are recorded in volumes of books, and they are the standard for all Muslims to follow.

Imam Musa al-Kazim

The son of al-Imam Jafar as-Sadiq, al-Imam Musa al-Kazim was born in 128 A.H. (745 A.D.) and lived for fifty-five years. A great deal of his time was spent in prison, and he was murdered by the notorious false caliph, Harun al-Rashid. However, the patience and forbearance of al-Imam Musa al-Kazim won over the heinous crimes of his torturers. His name *al-Kazim* means one who swallows down his anger.

He used to pray for great lengths of time throughout the night, so that his prayer would extend until the morning prayer. He then would continue praying until the sun rose. His patience in prayer was remarkable. He remained in prostration before Allah without raising his head for hours. While he was unable to establish religious institutions or address congregations as his father had done, since he was forbidden to do so by the tyrant rulers of that time, he quietly preached about Islam to his followers. His restraint of anger and his patience in the face of oppression and tyranny were the weapons which he left as a legacy for all to emulate.

Imam al-Hassan al-Askari

The father of Imam Mohammad al-Mahdi, Imam al-Hassan al-Askari was born in 232 A.H. (846 A.D.) and was martyred at the age of only twenty-eight. Unquestionably, his devotion to Allah and his self-restraint (sabr) were symbols of faith at its zenith.

Imprisoned by the unjust Abbasid government, he performed a miracle. He mellowed his jailers who were given instruction to torture him. When asked what happened, the jailers and their reinforcements could only say that they suddenly found themselves in a state of grace and began to worship, pray, and fast. When asked about this sudden change, they replied that observing the Imam fasting through the day and standing in prayer throughout the night without rest can only come from a just and pious man. That when the Imam looked at them they would shiver and echo a feeling never felt before. That feeling was one of faith. The Abbasids were enraged and threw the Imam to the wild animals. Another miracle took place. The Abbasids came back hoping the body was devoured but only to find that the Imam was steadfast (sabr) in prayer and the wild animals hovered around him in attention.

Imam al-Hassan al-Askari is a leader of patience and perseverance, and all who follow his example will reach Paradise.

Asiya

Like the prophets, there have emerged women who were prime examples of sabr. Among the most noteworthy of these women were: Asiya, Mary (Maryam), Khadijah, and Fatima.

"And Allah sets forth, as an example to those who believe, the wife of Pharaoh (Asiya): Behold she said: 'O my Lord! Build for me, in nearness to Thee, a mansion in the Garden, and save me from Pharaoh and his doings, and save me from those that do wrong.'" (Qur'an 66:11)

For Asiya to have persevered in her faith is remarkable given that the Pharaoh was a very wicked and arrogant man. As the wife of Pharaoh, she had all the glory and wealth at her disposal. But she refused this and, instead, sought the highest spiritual attainment through prayer to Allah.

Mary (Maryam)

"And Maryam the daughter of 'Imran, who guarded her chastity; and We breathed into (her body) of Our ruh; and she testified to the truth of the words of her Lord and of His Revelations, and was one of the devout (servants)." (Qur'an 66:12)

Even as Mary was falsely accused by the Jews as being unchaste, she endured in her purity and faith. She gave birth to Prophet Jesus, even though she was a virgin. Mary is the only female mentioned by name in the Qur'an. One of the chapters in the Qur'an bears her name. The term *"ruh"* is used above, as it is extremely dangerous to call this term "spirit," as Allah cannot be quantified by stating that He has a "spirit." Perhaps, for example, this *"ruh"* is the "power" of Allah, or some other attribute of the Almighty.

Muslims put Mary on the highest level of morality and ethics. The Qur'an reveals verses in which Prophet Jesus showed the utmost in humility and conduct towards his mother, Mary.

Mary had attained such a high spiritual level that the angels used to visit her in her prayers. Chastity (*'iffah*) was her special virtue. Allah has afforded Mary a special place among women:

"Behold! The angels said: 'O Maryam! Allah hath chosen thee and purified thee--chosen thee above the women of all nations. O Maryam! Worship thy Lord devoutly: prostrate thyself, and bow down (in prayer) with those who bow down.'" (Qur'an 3:42-43)

Khadijah

Khadijah was the first wife of Prophet Mohammad, and she was about fifteen years older than him. At the time of marriage, Khadijah was forty years of age as Prophet Mohammad was twenty-five years old. Prior to her marriage to Prophet Mohammad, she had been a widow who had inherited a great deal of wealth. She had employed Prophet Mohammad (not a Prophet at the time) to work for her. She developed a love and respect for the Prophet that finally led to their marriage.

Khadijah was the first woman convert to Prophet Mohammad's message of Islam, and she is the mother of Fatima (the wife of al-Imam Ali). She was a successful merchant, and she was a staunch supporter of Prophet Mohammad, particularly, in the early and most difficult years of his mission. During that time, Prophet Mohammad and his followers were being severely persecuted for adopting the new faith of Islam. Khadijah, at that time, showed great signs of endurance and perseverance as she stood by him in the worst of times. Khadijah died following twenty-five years of marriage to Prophet Mohammad. During that time, the Prophet Mohammad's life with her was an uninterrupted sunshine of happiness. Their daughter, Fatima, became the wife of al-Imam Ali.

Fatima

The daughter of Prophet Mohammad and Khadijah, and the wife of al-Imam Ali, she is known as *Fatima az-Zahra* ("Flower"). In their love and reverence for Fatima, the followers of the Prophet Mohammad proclaimed his daughter as the "Lady of Paradise" and "Our Lady of Light." She is the essence of womanhood, the purest of females, and the ideal standard for all Muslims to follow. She married al-Imam Ali of her own free will, having refused several others who had previously asked for her hand in marriage. This is an important point, for it shows that Prophet Mohammad allowed his daughter the right of choice.

Like her father, husband, and two sons, al-Imam Hassan and al-Imam Hussein, she, too, was in a state of purity. She was the purest of examples as daughter, wife, and mother. She excelled in the virtues of loyalty, kindness, gentleness, humility, and generosity. Her example of patience and constancy had distinguished her among the greatest of women, and she has been blessed with Allah bestowing upon her as the leader of women in Paradise. Like Mary she, too, communicated with angels. This is a very important point, since angels usually only communicate with prophets.

She had obtained from her father, Prophet Mohammad, the title of *Sayyidat Nisa' al-Alamin* ("Head of All Women of All Worlds"). The Prophet Mohammad had stated:

"The happiness of Fatima is my happiness and my happiness is the happiness of Allah. The anger of Fatima is my anger and my anger is the anger of Allah." (Prophet Mohammad)

Fatima had passed away several months after the death of her father, Prophet Mohammad. During her lifetime, she always sought the devotion of Allah over her own pleasures. What better example of sabr than when she spent practically all of her personal property for the cause of Allah. She even went hungry at times because she relinquished her food to the needy.

PART VII: ISLAMIC LEADERSHIP: A CASE EXAMPLE OF SABR

Aspect of Leadership

"Leadership" is a word on everyone's lips. Discussions on leadership are often as majestically useless as they are pretentious. Leadership is like the abominable snowman, whose footprints are everywhere but who is nowhere to be seen. Leadership is the process of moving a group (or groups) in some direction through mostly noncoercive means. Effective leadership is that which produces movement in the long-term best interests of the group (or groups). While this definition of leadership is appropriate for those who manage companies or businesses, we as Muslims need to link ourselves to another kind of leadership: spiritual or Islamic leadership.

Islamic Leadership:

Islamic leadership, also known as spiritual leadership, has a special place in the history of Islam. Notwithstanding that all the Prophets exhibited spiritual leadership, it is the point of this research to concentrate on spiritual leadership of one of the progeny of Prophet Mohammad.

Leadership Through al-Imam Hussein's Martyrdom

Leadership was put to the test during the period of Yazid's illegal rule. Al-Imam Hussein (grandson of Prophet Mohammad and son of al-Imam Ali and Fatima) fought and died for the protection of Islam. To him, Islam was not only threatened but on the verge of collapse and destruction. But threatened by whom? Many scholars believe it was a fight against Yazid, the false Caliph and tyrant, and his followers. A more in-depth analysis reveals that al-Imam Hussein's underlying mission was to put an end to those who compromised their Islamic values and ideals. What was compromised was the very essence of Islam.

At Karbala (city in Iraq), al-Imam Hussein fought and died for the sanctity of Islam. He addressed his followers with the following speech:

"Allah has, this day, permitted us to be engaged in a Holy War and He shall reward us for our martyrdom. So prepare yourselves to fight against the enemies of Islam with patience and resistance. O sons of the noble and self-respecting persons, be patient! Death is nothing but a bridge which you must cross after facing trials and tribulations so as to reach Heaven and its joys. Which of you does not like to go from this prison (world) to the lofty palaces (Paradise)?"

To this, his companions replied:

"O our Master! We are all ready to defend you and your Ahl al-Bayt, and to sacrifice our lives for the cause of Islam."

When al-Imam Hussein raised his sword for the first time on the battlefield, it was against the tyranny, oppression, and false leadership of Yazid and his followers.

When he raised his lance for the second time, it was a symbolic gesture against those so-called allies who broke their treaty with al-Imam Hussein and would not support his mission at Karbala, because they compromised their Islamic values and ideals.

When al-Imam Hussein raised his lance for the third time, it was a message to those so-called Muslim friends and relatives who stayed home and awaited the outcome of the battle before declaring their allegiance to support either al-Imam Hussein or the enemy. And this al-Imam Hussein saw as a compromise.

When he raised his sword for the fourth time, it was the most horrible moment in his life. In his vision, al-Imam Hussein saw the danger when Muslims in the centuries to follow would, likewise, compromise their Islamic values and ideals. Al-Imam Hussein had to do something about it. He gave his life so that we can reflect on those horrid days at Karbala and, more importantly, upon our own situation in contemporary times to understand that we, too, have compromised our own Islamic values and ideals, perhaps, even far worse than those Muslims did during al-Imam Hussein's time.

For al-Imam Hussein, he was the essence of sabr, because he was firm in his purpose, maintained his consciousness of Allah (*taqwah*), and chose the straight path leading to his ultimate sacrifice to save Islam. What he left at Karbala was the example. And the very essence of that example was prayer. His perseverance in prayer at Karbala was the light that drew even some of the enemies to his side at that time. While al-Imam Hussein and his tiny contingent were in prayer, some of the opposition such as the well-known soldier, Hurr, were so drawn to the true believers that they crossed over and joined them.

It is important to understand that it was the prayer which al-Imam Hussein was safeguarding. He saw that Muslims were compromising their prayer. Make no mistake about this, the enemies at Karbala also prayed. But the prayers by the enemies were null and void. Can one pray and then proceed to murder the grandson of the Prophet Mohammad? No! So you see even prayer was distorted, and the reason was that the enemies lacked sabr in their prayer, and they had fallen from the straight path.

Al-Imam Hussein's message is for people not to compromise Islam, and to realize that one's salvation is through the practice of sabr and prayer. Seeking knowledge, understanding, and wisdom, or striving towards prosperity and tranquillity, cannot be meaningful without the security of the foundation of faith. That security is the prayer. While it is important to seek knowledge and understanding, for example, these needs in Islam are nurtured in self-awareness once prayer is solidified.

The centuries following al-Imam Hussein's martyrdom saw Muslims time and time again compromising their Islamic values and ideals. Whether with the Umayyads, the Abbasids, or in contemporary times, we note that Islam for Muslims is being threatened throughout the world. Many Muslim countries, for example, grant fewer religious freedoms to their subjects than do leaders of Western nations. The problem here is deep-rooted; it is a problem of the Muslims themselves. In order to assimilate into the mainstream of a non-Islamic society, Muslims often feel it necessary to forego their Islamic traditions, lifestyles, and behavior in order to be accepted by that society. As stated earlier, these Muslims have fallen to the lowest form of degradation for they have substituted Islam for convenience and social compatibility.

Sabr applies to the best of times as well as to the worst of times. While wealth and prosperity are great blessings, they are also, at the same time, great trials of faith:

"And if We cause him to taste of great blessing after misfortune has befallen him, he says: 'all evil has departed from me:' Behold, he becomes exultant and boastful, except for those who have patience and do good works. Theirs will be forgiveness and a great reward." (Qur'an 11:10-11)

Let us reflect on the martyrdom of al-Imam Hussein and learn from his example. Remember that Islam cannot be compromised. To know whether or not you have compromised Islam requires that you have knowledge of at least the basic fundamentals of Islam. This requires an understanding of what Islam is and what it is not. When you submit your will to Allah, be certain of your faith, believe in al-Imam Hussein's message, and accept the challenge that you will strive in the way of Allah to better yourself as a Muslim. Be steadfast and actionable in your obligation to Islam. Display the right attitude so that your faith can endure. Let your behavior be one for others to follow, and above all be patient!

EPILOGUE

Sabr is the key to a better understanding of our roles as Muslims. Sabr shapes and molds the way we behave and act. Our very lifestyles must depend on sabr if we are to achieve Allah's Compassion and Mercy.

Sabr is a more active and dynamic term than the word patience as defined in an English dictionary. For Muslims, patience is proactive, and it has many definitions and characteristics. Literally, sabr means to tie down our uncontrolled fears, passions, and weaknesses. Sabr has many meanings. Sabr implies patience not hastiness. Sabr also means perseverance, constancy, steadfastness, and determination.

We need patience to bear the assaults of the devil and to persevere in our faith. Patience weeps tears of comfort and finds content in the midst of discontent. Patience turns bitterness into sweetness. Human endurance is a part of a fabric of virtues which leads to faith in the love of Allah. Seek Allah's help in hardship and calamity with patience and perseverance. This help is sought through prayer which strengthens and reinforces the power of patience and perseverance. This power derives from the miracle of prayer, because through sabr we can attain enlightenment through our self-concept, self-esteem, and self-fulfillment. This enlightenment results in contentment and happiness.

The power of sabr is more than a miracle. Sabr reaches its highest level when a person is faced with adversities and calamities, is threatened with the loss of life and property, and sees no hope. Here, man exercises his sabr in light of his sufferings, and submits his complete will to Allah. Prophet Job showed us that true patience is a mark of the just. Patience is a virtue which enables one to bear all adversity that can befall him, and he does this with constant resolution. Sabr brings about the Pleasure of Allah. Allah wishes that we develop this power in order to defeat both internal and external forces hostile to truth. Prayer builds up our endurance for hardship, and true Muslims become tolerant through their daily prayers.

It is with the quality of sabr that man declares himself satisfied with Allah's Pleasure. Sabr is the armor by which one defends his soul. With sabr we strive towards becoming closer to Allah: His Obedience and Devotion as well as His Compassion and Mercy. We seek this nearness to Allah even in the face of calamities, disasters, difficulties, and hardships. We work towards perseverance in the face of these misfortunes and adversities. We seek out the pious and join with them in pleasing Allah. With sabr we refrain from those things which displease

Allah. Sabr applies both to the worst of times as well as to the best of times.

Beyond our human ability, there is a higher order, Divine Wisdom, that we are not able to fully understand. However, we seek His Truth, Knowledge, Understanding, and Wisdom in order to obtain self-realization as Muslims.

Both believers and unbelievers are troubled with calamities in the life of this world. Allah has His way of dealing with both types. He does this by testing us. Calamities and hardships are means by which Allah tests the purity and seriousness of our faith. Testing is a part of the verification of our faith. Patience is the energetic power of faith. Those who were tested the most as to patience were the Prophets and those who are closer to Allah. We are tested by the good fortunes in life as well as by the misfortunes in life. One should not seek calamity or disaster, but if it befalls him he should persevere in his patience to endure this difficulty.

We should not torture ourselves to obtain sabr. For example, breaking one's Ramadan fast several hours after *iftar* (breakfast) is not desirable and does not gain Allah's Mercy. Even when one meets the enemy on a battlefield, he should not be too eager to fight. Here, it is far better to ask Allah for His Guidance and Tranquillity in order to pave the way for reconciliation and peace. But if you have to face the enemy, then do so by practicing patience, perseverance, and resolution.

Sabr is related to many virtues: Allah's Forgiveness, Gratitude, Confidence, Dependence, and Trust as well as His Compassion and Mercy. Sabr is a virtue for all occasions. The essence of sabr comes from Allah, Who not only commands patience, but also is Himself Patient. There is a double reward for the believers who practice sabr: Paradise and garments of silk. These believers attain the highest place in Paradise because of their patience and perseverance. Sabr is the light for the believers, and it is equal to the value of half of one's faith.

How we attain sabr is by strengthening our faith in Allah even in the face of calamity. Everything decreed by Allah was known by Allah even before the earth was created. We need to strive towards removing our unnecessary anxieties and fears. We should not rush or demand solutions for our adversities. With every difficulty there is relief. Every difficulty we face in life could be atonement for our sins. We must turn to Allah and ask for His Guidance in the face of any hardship. Endure in that hardship no matter how severe by strengthening our resolve and patience. Here, the triumph of patience leads to self-fulfillment.

103

The first draft of this book was written in the month of Ramadan in the Islamic year 1414 (February-March, 1994). With Allah's Blessing, this book will be an inspiration to all who seek to better understand themselves and their metaphysical relationship with Allah. It was only through patience and perseverance (sabr) that this book was begun and completed.

APPENDIX

Qur'anic Verses: Sabr

"Nay, seek (Allah's) help with patient perseverance and prayer: It is indeed hard, except to those who bring a lowly spirit." (Qur'an 2:45)

"And remember ye said: 'O Moses! We cannot endure one kind of food (always); so beseech thy Lord for us to produce for us of what the earth groweth, its pot-herbs, and cucumbers, its garlic, lentils, and onions.' He said: 'Will ye exchange the better for the worse? Go ye down to any town, and ye shall find what ye want!' They were covered with humiliation and misery; they drew on themselves the wrath of Allah. This because they went on rejecting the Signs of Allah and slaying His Messengers without just cause. This because they rebelled and went on transgressing." (Qur'an 2:61)

"O ye who believe! Seek help with patient perseverance and prayer: for Allah is with those who patiently persevere." (Qur'an 2:153)

"Be sure we shall test you with something of fear and hunger, some loss in goods or lives or the fruits (of your toil), but give glad tidings to those who patiently persevere." (Qur'an 2:155)

"They are the ones who buy Error in place of Guidance and Torment in place of Forgiveness. Ah! What boldness (they show) for the Fire!" (Qur'an 2:175)

"It is not righteousness that ye turn your faces towards East or West; but it is righteousness to believe in Allah and the Last Day, and the Angels, and the Book, and the Messengers; to spend of your substance, out of love for Him, for your kin, for orphans, for the needy, for the wayfarer, for those who ask, and for the ransom of slaves; to be steadfast in prayer, and practice regular charity; to fulfill the contracts which ye have made; and to be firm and patient, in pain (or suffering) and adversity, and throughout all periods of panic. Such are the people of truth, the Allah-fearing." (Qur'an 2:177)

"When Talut set forth with the armies, he said: 'Allah will test you at the stream: if any drinks of its water, he goes not with my army; only those who taste not of it go with me: a mere sip out of the hand is excused.' But they all drank of it, except a few. When they crossed the river, he and the faithful ones with him, they said: 'This day we cannot cope with Goliath and his forces.' But those who were convinced that they must meet Allah, said: 'How oft, by Allah's will, hath a small force vanquished a big one? Allah is with those who steadfastly persevere.'" (Qur'an 2:249)

"When they advanced to meet Goliath and his forces, they prayed: 'Our Lord! Pour out constancy on us and make our steps firm: help us against those that reject faith.'" (Qur'an 2:250)

"Those who show patience, firmness and self-control; who are true (in word and deed); who worship devoutly; who spend (in the way of Allah); and who pray for forgiveness in the early hours of the morning." (Qur'an 3:17)

"If aught that is good befalls you, it grieves them; but if some misfortune overtakes you, they rejoice at it. But if ye are constant and do right, not the least harm will their cunning do to you; for Allah compasseth round about all that they do." (Qur'an 3:120)

"'Yea, if ye remain firm, and act aright, even if the enemy should rush here on you in hot haste, your Lord would help you with five thousand angels making a terrific onslaught.'" (Qur'an 3:125)

"Did ye think that ye would enter Heaven without Allah testing those of you who fought hard (in His Cause) and remained steadfast?" (Qur'an 3:142)

"How many of the Prophets fought (in Allah's way), and with them (fought) large bands of godly men? But they never lost heart if they met with disaster in Allah's way, nor did they weaken (in will) nor give in. And Allah loves those who are firm and steadfast." (Qur'an 3:146)

"Ye shall certainly be tried and tested in your possessions and in your personal selves; and ye shall certainly hear much that will grieve you, from those who received the Book before you and from those who worship many gods. But if ye persevere patiently, and guard against evil, then that will be a determining factor in all affairs." (Qur'an 3:186)

"O ye who believe! Persevere in patience and constancy; vie in such perseverance; strengthen each other; and fear Allah; that ye may prosper." (Qur'an 3:200)

"If any of you have not the means wherewith to wed free believing women, they may wed believing girls from among those whom your right hands possess: and Allah hath full knowledge about your Faith. Ye are one from another: wed them with the leave of their owners, and give them their dowers, according to what is reasonable: they should be chaste, not lustful, nor taking paramours: when they are taken in wedlock, if they fall into shame, their punishment is half that for free women. This (permission) is for those among you who fear sin; but it is better for you that ye practice self-restraint. And Allah is Oft-Forgiving, Most Merciful." (Qur'an 4:25)

"Rejected were the Apostles before thee: with patience and constancy they bore their rejection and their wrongs, until Our aid did reach them: there is none that can alter the Words (and Decrees) of Allah. Already hast thou received some account of those Apostles." (Qur'an 6:34)

"'And if there is a party among you who believes in the Message with which I have been sent, and a party which does not believe, hold yourselves in patience until Allah doth decide between us: for He is the best to decide.'" (Qur'an 7:87)

"'But those dost wreak thy vengeance on us simply because we believed in the Signs of our Lord when they reached us! Our Lord! Pour out on us patience and constancy, and take our souls unto Thee as Muslims (who bow to Thy Will)!'" (Qur'an 7:126)

"Said Moses to his people: 'Pray for help from Allah, and (wait) in patience and constancy: for the earth is Allah's, to give as a heritage to such of His servants as He pleaseth; and the end is (best) for the righteous.'" (Qur'an 7:128)

"And We made a people, considered weak (and of no account), inheritors of lands in both East and West, lands whereon We sent down Our blessings. The fair promise of thy Lord was fulfilled for the Children of Israel, because they had patience and constancy, and We leveled to the ground the great works and fine buildings which Pharaoh and his people erected (with such pride)." (Qur'an 7:137)

"And obey Allah and His Apostle; and fall into no disputes, lest ye lose heart and your power depart; and be patient and persevering; for Allah is with those who patiently persevere." (Qur'an 8:46)

"O Apostle! Rouse the Believers to the fight. If there are twenty amongst you, patient and persevering, they will vanquish two hundred: if a hundred, they will vanquish a thousand of the Unbelievers: for these are a people without understanding." (Qur'an 8:65)

"For the present, Allah hath lightened your (task), for He knoweth that there is a weak spot in you: but (even so), if there are a hundred of you, patient and persevering, they will vanquish two hundred, and if a thousand, they will vanquish two thousand, with the leave of Allah: for Allah is with those who patiently persevere." (Qur'an 8:66)

"Follow thou the inspiration sent unto thee, and be patient and constant, till Allah does decide: for He is the Best to decide." (Qur'an 10:109)

"Not so do those who show patience and constancy, and work righteousness; for them is forgiveness (of sins) and a great reward." (Qur'an 11:11)

"Such are some of the stories of the Unseen, which We have revealed unto thee: before this, neither thou nor thy People knew them. So persevere patiently: for the End is for those who are righteous." (Qur'an 11:49)

"And be steadfast in patience; for verily Allah will not suffer the reward of the righteous to perish." (Qur'an 11:115)

"They stained his shirt with false blood. He said: 'Nay, but your minds have made up a tale (that may pass) with you. (For me) patience is most fitting: against that which ye assert, it is Allah (alone) whose help can be sought.'" (Qur'an 12:18)

"Jacob said: 'Nay, but ye have yourselves contrived a story (good enough) for you. So patience is most fitting (for me). Maybe Allah will bring them (back) all to me (in the end). For He is indeed full of Knowledge and Wisdom.'" (Qur'an 12:83)

"They said: 'Art thou indeed Joseph?' He said, 'I am Joseph, and this is my brother: Allah has indeed been gracious to us (all): behold, he that is righteous and patient, never will Allah suffer the reward to be lost, of those who do right.'" (Qur'an 12:90)

"Those who patiently persevere, seeking the countenance of their Lord; establish regular prayers; spend, out of (the gifts) We have bestowed for their sustenance, secretly and openly; and turn off Evil with Good: for such there is the final attainment of the (Eternal) Home." (Qur'an 13:22)

"'Peace unto you for that ye persevered in patience! Now how excellent is the final Home!'" (Qur'an 13:24)

"We sent Moses with Our Signs (and the command). 'Bring out thy people from the depths of darkness into light, and teach them to remember the Days of Allah.' Verily in this there are Signs for such as are firmly patient and constant, grateful and appreciative." (Qur'an 14:5)

"'No reason have we why we should not put our trust on Allah. Indeed He has guided us to the ways we (follow). We shall certainly bear with patience all the hurt you may cause us. For those who put their trust should put their trust on Allah.'" (Qur'an 14:12)

"They will all be marshaled before Allah together: then will the weak say to those who were arrogant, 'For us, we but followed you; can ye then avail us at all against the Wrath of Allah?' They will reply, 'If we

had received the guidance of Allah, we should have given it to you: to us it makes no difference (now) whether we rage, or bear (these torments) with patience: for ourselves there is no way of escape.'" (Qur'an 14:21)

"(They are) those who persevere in patience, and put their trust on their Lord." (Qur'an 16:42)

"What is with you must vanish: what is with Allah will endure, and We will certainly bestow on those who patiently persevere, their reward according to the best of their actions." (Qur'an 16:96)

"But verily thy Lord, to those who leave their homes after trials and persecutions, and who thereafter strive and fight for the Faith and patiently persevere, thy Lord, after all this is Oft-Forgiving, Most Merciful." (Qur'an 16:110)

"And if ye do catch them out, catch them out no worse than they catch you out: but if ye show patience, that is indeed the best (course) for those who are patient." (Qur'an 16:126)

"And do thou be patient, for thy patience is but from Allah; nor grieve over them: and distress not thyself because of their plots." (Qur'an 16:127)

"And keep thy soul content with those who call on their Lord morning and evening, seeking His Wujah; and let not thine eyes pass beyond them, seeking the pomp and glitter of this Life; nor obey any whose heart We have permitted to neglect the remembrance of Us, one who follows his own desires, whose case has gone beyond all bounds." (Qur'an 18:28)

"(The other) said: 'Verily thou wilt not be able to have patience with me!'" (Qur'an 18:67)

"'And how canst thou have patience about things about which thy understanding is not complete?'" (Qur'an 18:68)

"Moses said: 'Thou wilt find me, if Allah so wills, (truly) patient: nor shall I disobey thee in aught." (Qur'an 18:69)

"He answered: 'Did I not tell thee that thou canst have no patience with me?'" (Qur'an 18:72)

"He answered: 'Did I not tell thee that thou canst have no patience with me?'" (Qur'an 18:75)

"He answered: 'This is the parting between me and thee: now will I tell thee the interpretation of (those things) over which thou was unable to hold patience.'" (Qur'an 18:78)

"'As for the wall, it belonged to two youths, orphans, in the town; there was, beneath it, a buried treasure, to which they were entitled; their father had been a righteous man: so thy Lord desired that they should attain their age of full strength and get out their treasure - a mercy (and favor) from thy Lord. I did it not of my own accord. Such is the interpretation of (those things) over which thou was unable to hold patience.'" (Qur'an 18:82)

"'Lord of the heavens and of the earth, and of all that is between them: so worship Him, and be constant and patient in His worship: knowest thou of any who is worthy of the same Name as He?'" (Qur'an 19:65)

"Therefore be patient with what they say, and celebrate (constantly) the praises of thy Lord, before the rising of the sun, and before its setting; yea, celebrate them for part of the hours of the night, and at the sides of the day: that thou mayest have (spiritual) joy." (Qur'an 20:130)

"Enjoin prayer on thy people, and be constant therein. We ask thee not to provide sustenance: We provide it for thee. But the (fruit of) the Hereafter is for Righteousness." (Qur'an 20:132)

"And (remember) Ismail, Idris, and Zul-kifl, all (men) of constancy and patience." (Qur'an 21:85)

"To those whose hearts, when Allah is mentioned, are filled with fear, who show patient perseverance over their afflictions, keep up regular prayer, and spend (in charity) out of what we have bestowed upon them." (Qur'an 22:35)

"'I have rewarded them this day for their patience and constancy: they are indeed the ones that have achieved Bliss.'" (Qur'an 23:111)

"And the Apostles whom We sent before thee were all (Men) who ate food and walked through the streets: We have made some of you as a trial for others: will ye have patience? For Allah is One Who Sees (all things)." (Qur'an 25:20)

"'He indeed would well-nigh have misled us from our gods, had it not been that we were constant to them!' Soon will they know, when they see the Penalty, who it is that is most misled in Path!" (Qur'an 25:42)

"Those are the ones who will be rewarded with the highest place in Heaven, because of their patient constancy: therein shall they be met with salutations and peace." (Qur'an 25:75)

"Twice will they be given their reward, for that they have persevered, that they avert Evil with Good, and that they spend (in charity) out of what We have given them." (Qur'an 28:54)

"But those who had been granted (true) knowledge said: 'Alas for you! The reward of Allah (in the Hereafter) is best for those who believe and work righteousness: but this none shall attain, save those who steadfastly persevere (in good).'" (Qur'an 28:80)

"Those who persevere in patience, and put their trust in their Lord and Cherisher." (Qur'an 29:59)

"So patiently persevere: for verily the promise of Allah is true: nor let those shake thy firmness, who have (themselves) no certainty of faith." (Qur'an 30:60)

"'O my son! Establish regular prayer, enjoin what is just, and forbid what is wrong: and bear with patient constancy whatever betide thee; for this is firmness (of purpose) in (the conduct of) affairs." (Qur'an 31:17)

"Seest thou not that the ships sail through the ocean by the grace of Allah? That He may show you of His Signs? Verily in this are Signs for all who constantly persevere and give thanks." (Qur'an 31:31)

"And We appointed, from among them, leaders, giving guidance under Our command, so long as they persevered with patience and continued to have faith in Our Signs." (Qur'an 32:24)

"For Muslim men and women, for believing men and women, for devout men and women, for true men and women, for men and women who are patient and constant, for men and women who humble themselves, for men and women who give in charity, for men and women who fast (and deny themselves), for men and women who guard their chastity, and for men and women who engage much in Allah's praise, for them has Allah prepared forgiveness and great reward." (Qur'an 33:35)

"But they said: 'Our Lord! Place longer distances between our journey-stages:' But they wronged themselves (therein). At length We made them as a tale (that is told), and We dispersed them all in scattered fragments. Verily in this are Signs for every (soul that is) patiently constant and grateful." (Qur'an 34:19)

"Then, when (the son) reached (the age of) (serious) work with him, he said: 'O my son! I see in vision that I offer thee in sacrifice: now see what is thy view!' (The son) said: 'O my father! Do as thou art commanded: thou will find me, if Allah so wills one practicing patience and constancy!'" (Qur'an 37:102)

"And the leaders among them go away (impatiently), (saying), 'Walk ye away, and remain constant to your gods! For this is truly a thing designed (against you)!'" (Qur'an 38:6)

"Have patience at what they say, and remember Our servant, David, the man of strength: for he ever turned (to Allah)." (Qur'an 38:17)

"'And take in thy hand a little grass, and strike therewith: and break not (thy oath).' Truly We found him full of patience and constancy. How excellent in Our service! Ever did he turn (to Us)!" (Qur'an 38:44)

"Say: 'O ye My servants who believe! Fear your Lord. Good is (the reward) for those who do good in this world. Spacious is Allah's earth! Those who patiently persevere will truly receive a reward without measure!" (Qur'an 39:10)

"Patiently, then, persevere: for the Promise of Allah is true: and ask forgiveness for thy fault, and celebrate the Praises of thy Lord in the evening and in the morning." (Qur'an 40:55)

"So persevere in patience; for the Promise of Allah is true: and whether We show thee (in this life) some part of what We promise them, or We take thy soul (to Our Mercy) (before that), (in any case) it is to Us that they shall (all) return." (Qur'an 40:77)

"If, then, they have patience, the Fire will be a Home for them! And if they beg to be received into favor, into favor will they not (then) be received." (Qur'an 41:24)

"And no one will be granted such goodness except those who exercise patience and self-restraint, none but persons of the greatest good fortune." (Qur'an 41:35)

"If it be His Will, He can still the Wind: then would they become motionless on the back of the (ocean). Verily in this are Signs for everyone who patiently perseveres and is grateful." (Qur'an 42:33)

"But indeed if any show patience and forgive, that would truly be an exercise of courageous will and resolution in the conduct of affairs." (Qur'an 42:43)

"Therefore, patiently persevere, as did (all) Apostles of inflexible purpose; and be in no haste about the (Unbelievers). On the Day that they see the (Punishment) promised them, (it will be) as if they had not tarried more than an hour in a single day. (Thine but) to proclaim the Message: but shall any be destroyed except those who transgress?" (Qur'an 46:35)

"And We shall try you until We test those among you who strive their utmost and persevere in patience; and We shall try your reported (mettle)." (Qur'an 47:31)

"If only they had patience until thou couldst come out to them, it would be best for them: but Allah is Oft-Forgiving, Most Merciful." (Qur'an 49:5)

"Bear, then, with patience, all that they say, and celebrate the Praises of thy Lord, before the rising of the sun and before (its) setting." (Qur'an 50:39)

"'Burn ye therein: the same is it to you whether ye bear it with patience, or not: ye but receive the recompense of your (own) deeds.'" (Qur'an 52:16)

"Now await in patience the command of thy Lord: for verily thou art in Our 'Ainah: and celebrate the Praises of thy Lord the while thou standest forth." (Qur'an 52:48)

"For We will send the she-camel by way of trial for them. So watch them, (O Salih), and possess thyself in patience!" (Qur'an 54:27)

"So wait with patience for the Command of thy Lord, and be not like the Companion of the Fish, when he cried out in agony." (Qur'an 68:48)

"Therefore, do thou hold patience - a patience of beautiful (contentment)." (Qur'an 70:5)

"And have patience with what they say, and leave them with noble (dignity)." (Qur'an 73:10)

"But, for thy Lord's (Cause), be patient and constant!" (Qur'an 74:7)

"And because they were patient and constant, He will reward them with a Garden and (garments of) silk." (Qur'an 76:12)

"Therefore, be patient with constancy to the Command of thy Lord, and hearken not to the sinner or the ingrate among them." (Qur'an 76:24)

"Then will he be of those who believe, and enjoin patience (constancy, and self-restraint), and enjoin deeds of kindness and compassion." (Qur'an 90:17)

"Except such as have Faith, and do Righteous Deeds, and (join together) in the mutual teaching of Truth, and of Patience and Constancy." (Qur'an 103:3)

113

Source: Ali, Abdullah Yusuf. *The Holy Qur'an: Text, Translation and Commentary*, 1934.

Occurrence of Sabr in the Qur'an

Derivative	Chapter	Verse
Sabara	Shura	42:43
	Ahqaf	46:35
Sabartum	Ra'ad	13:24
	Nahl	16:126
Sabarna	Ibrahim	14:21
	Furqan	25:42
Sabaru	An'am	6:34
	A'raf	7:137
	Hud	11:11
	Ra'd	13:22
	Nahl	16:42
	Nahl	16:96
	Nahl	16:110
	Mu'minun	23:111
	Furqan	25:75
	Qasas	28:54
	Ankabut	29:59
	Sajda	32:24
	Fussilat	41:35
	Hujurat	49:5
	Insan	76:12
Tasbir	Kahf	18:68
Tasbiru	Al-i-Imran	3:120
	Al-i-Imran	3:125
	Al-i-Imran	3:186
	Nisaa	4:25
	Tur	52:16
Astasbirun	Furqan	25:20
Nasbir	Baqara	2:61
Walanasbiran	Ibrahim	14:12

Yasbir	Yusuf	12:90
Yasbiru	Fussilat	41:24
Isbir	Yunus	10:109
	Hud	11:49
	Hud	11:115
	Nahl	16:127
	Kahf	18:28
	Ta-Ha	20:130
	Rum	30:60
	Luqman	31:17
	Sad	38:17
	Mu'min	40:55
	Mu'min	40:77
	Ahqaf	46:35
	Qaf	50:39
	Tur	52:48
	Qalam	68:48
	Ma'arij	70:5
	Muzzammil	73:10
	Muddaththir	74:7
	Insan	76:2
Isbiru	Al-i-Imran	3:200
	A'raf	7:87
	A'raf	7:128
	Anfal	8:46
	Sad	38:6
	Tur	52:16
Sabiru	Al-i-Imran	3:200
Ma-asbaruhum	Baqara	2:175
Istabir	Maryam	19:65
	Ta-Ha	20:132
	Qamar	54:27
Alsabir	Baqara	2:45
	Baqara	2:153

	Yusuf	12:18
	Yusuf	12:83
	Balad	90:17
	Asr	103:3
Sabran	Baqara	2:250
	A'raf	7:126
	Kahf	18:67
	Kahf	18:72
	Kahf	18:75
	Kahf	18:78
	Kahf	18:82
	Ma'arij	70:5
Sabrak	Nahl	16:127
Sabiran	Kahf	18:69
	Sad	38:44
Alsabirun	Anfal	8:65
	Qasas	28:80
	Zumar	39:10
Alsabireen	Baqara	2:153
	Baqara	2:155
	Baqara	2:177
	Baqara	2:249
	Al-i-Imran	3:17
	Al-i-Imran	3:142
	Al-i-Imran	3:146
	Anfal	8:46
	Anfal	8:66
	Nahl	16:126
	Anbiyaa	21:85
	Hajj	22:35
	Ahzab	33:35
	Saffat	37:102
	Mohammad	47:31
Sabirah	Anfal	8:66
Alsabirat	Ahzab	33:35

117

Sabbar	Ibrahim	14:5
	Luqman	31:31
	Saba	34:19
	Shura	42:33

Source: Data derived from *Al-Mu'jam al-Mufahrus (Encyclopedia Index of Qur'anic Words)*, Second Edition, 1988, written by Mohammad Fuad Abdul-Baki, Cairo, Egypt, Dar al-Hadith (publisher).

GLOSSARY

'Adil	Just
'Ain	Perception
'Asr	Afternoon
'Iffah	Chastity
'Ilm	Knowledge
'Isha	Early Night
'Umra	Informal Pilgrimage
Abideen	Lord of the Worshippers
Ada'	Adherence
Ahl al-Bayt	Members of the Family of Prophet Mohammad
Amal	Action
Aman an-Nafs	Self-Security
Amr-Bil-Ma'aroof	Enjoin Good
Ananiyah	Egoism
Anbiya	Prophets
Asas an-Nafs	Self-Foundation
Asmau'l-Husna	Beautiful Names of Allah
Ayat	Verses
Ayoub	Job
Barzagh	Partition
Dawood	David
Enarat	Enlightenment
Enfial	Emotion
Fahim	Understanding
Fajr	Dawn
Falah	Prosperity
Farah	Happiness
Fitra	Charity in Ramadan
Furu' al-Din	Branches of Faith
Ghusl	Washing
Hadith	Traditional Statements by Prophet Mohammad
Hajj	Formal Pilgrimage
Halal	Allowable
Halim	Forbearance
Haq	Truth
Haram	Forbidden
Hayat	Life

Hikma	Wisdom
Hilm	Gentleness
Ibada	Worship
Idrak an-Nafs	Self-Realization
Iftar	Breakfast
Ihtiram	Respect
Ikhlas	Devotion
Ikrar	Acceptance
Imam	Leader; Chief
Imamah	Succession of Prophet Mohammad
Iman	Faith
Infaq	Generosity
Injeel	Gospel
Ismail	Ishmael
Israfeel	Angel Who Blows Trumpet on Final Day
Izraeel	Angel of Death
Jibraeel	Angel Gabriel
Jihad al-Akbar	Major Struggle
Jihad al-Azghar	Minor Struggle
Jihad	Struggle
Ka'bah	Holy Shrine in Mecca
Kazim	Restrains Anger
Khalil	Friend
Khalq	Creation
Khulood	Eternity
Khulq	Morals
Khums	One-Fifth
Kitab-al-Munir	Book of Enlightenment
Kurbatan Illallah	Nearness to Allah
Kutub	Books
Libas	Garment
Ma'ad	Resurrection
Maghrib	Evening
Makruh	Reprehensible; Undesirable
Malaika	Angels
Maryam	Mary
Masjid	Place of Worship
Mawkaf	Attitude
Mawt	Death
Miftah al-Faraj	Key of Relief
Mikaeel	Angel Michael

Mubah	Allowable
Munir	Enlighten
Mustahabb	Desirable
Nafs	Individual Self; Human Soul
Nafs Ammarah	Evil Soul
Nafs Lawwamah	Reproving Soul
Nafs Mutma'innah	Tranquil Soul
Nahi-Anil-Munkar	Prohibit Evil
Najis	Impure
Natthafa	Cleanliness
Ni'ma	Blessing
Nisa'	Women
Nitham	Cosmos (Order and Harmony)
Qana'a	Contentment
Qur'an	Holy Book of Islam
Rab	Lord
Rahman	Beneficent
Ramadan	Month of Fasting
Retha an-Nafs	Self-Satisfaction
Riba	Usury
Rikat	Part
Ruh	Spirit (Human Beings)
Sabara	Bind; Tie
Sabr	Patience; Endurance; Constancy
Sabur	Patient
Sadaka	Charity
Sakina	Tranquillity
Salat al-Jama'ah	Group Prayer
Salat	Prayer
Salihat	Righteous Deeds
Salwan	Comfort
Sayyidat Nisa' al-Alamin	Head of Women of All Worlds
Shahadah	Declaration of Faith
Shaja'a	Courage
Shakur	Appreciative
Sharaf	Honor
Shari'ah	Law
Shukr	Gratitude
Sirat al-Mustakim	Straight Path
Siyam	Fasting
Sulook	Behavior
Sunnah	Lifestyle of Prophet Mohammad

Taharah	Purification
Tahkeek an-Nafs	Self-Achievement
Talut	King Saul
Taqwah	Piety
Tasdeek	Believing
Taslime	Submission
Tawakkul	Reliance
Taurat	Torah
Tazkiya	Self-Refinement
Thawab	Reward
Ulama	Religious Leaders
Ummah	People
Usul al-Din	Articles of Faith
Uzair	Ezra
Waee an-Nafs	Self-Awareness
Wajib	Duty
Wazir	Minister
Wudu'	Ablution
Yacoub	Jacob
Yakine	Certainty
Yawm al-Qiyamah	Day of Judgment
Zahra	Flower
Zakat	Alms
Zuboor	Psalms
Zuhd	Abstinence
Zuhr	Noon